MOTIVATE HER

FROM BEST SELLING AUTHOR

MOTIVATE HER

Empowering Women To Build Their Business
Empires & Become Financially Independent

CELESTE BELLWOOD

© 2023 by Celeste Bellwood

All rights reserved. No portion of this book may be reproduced, stored in retrieval system, or transmitted in any form or by any means – electronic, mechanical, photocopy, recording, scanning, or other – except for brief questions in critical reviews or articles, without the prior written permission of the publisher or author.

ISBN: 979-8-9884084-2-0 (Print)

Published by Celeste Bellwood. Celeste Bellwood's titles may be purchased in bulk for educational, business, fundraising, or sales promotional use. For information, please email hello@celestebellwood.com

First print edition: 2023

Celeste Bellwood

Motivate Her is the ambitious woman's roadmap to business success. Demystifying million-dollar brand building and offering insights into marketing psychology, this guide is more than a manual—it's a masterclass. Dive in to transform your entrepreneurial aspirations into reality

To the tenacious women charting their own courses, may this be the wind beneath your entrepreneurial wings.

TABLE OF CONTENTS

Introduction - pg. 11

Chapter 1: The Female Advantage - pg. 16
- Understanding the unique qualities and strengths women bring to the business world.
- Addressing and debunking common misconceptions.

Chapter 2: The Foundation of a Million-Dollar Brand - pg. 23
- Discovering your passion and purpose.
- Crafting a vision and mission statement.
- Brand differentiation and USP (Unique Selling Proposition).

Chapter 3: Brand Aesthetics and Identity - pg. 38
- Importance of a cohesive look and feel.
- Case studies of popular brands that nailed their aesthetic.

Chapter 4: The Psychology of Marketing and Branding - pg. 54
- Dive into human behavior, emotion, and persuasion.
- Cognitive biases and how they play into marketing.

Chapter 5: Mastering Social Media Marketing - pg. 67
- An overview of top platforms (Instagram, LinkedIn, TikTok, Facebook, etc.).
- Developing content strategies for each platform.
- Leveraging ads and organic growth.

Chapter 6: Building an Authentic Community - pg. 85
- The importance of engagement.
- Case studies of brands that have a loyal customer base.
- Building trust and credibility.

TABLE OF CONTENTS

Chapter 7: Effective Networking and Partnerships - pg. 101
- Leveraging connections to expand reach.
- Collaborative marketing and brand partnerships.

Chapter 8: Financial Intelligence and Management - pg. 113
- Understanding cash flow, profit margins, and ROI.
- Importance of financial planning and seeking expert advice.

Chapter 9: Scaling and Expansion - pg. 129
- When and how to scale.
- Expansion strategies, from franchising to mergers.

Chapter 10: Overcoming Adversity - pg. 143
- Personal stories of challenges I've faced.
- Resilience-building techniques.

Chapter 11: The Power of Continuous Learning - pg. 153
- Keeping up with industry trends and changes.
- Recommended resources and courses.

Chapter 12: Women in Leadership - pg. 163

Chapter 13: AI For Business - pg. 171

Chapter 14: Maintaining Work-Life Balance - pg. 184
- The challenge of juggling business with personal life.
- Maintaining mental and emotional well-being.

Chapter 15: The Future of Women in Business - pg. 194
- Predictions and aspirations for the next generation of female entrepreneurs.
- How to be a mentor and give back to the community.

Conclusion, Challenges, & Tips - pg. 207

INTRODUCTION

Every great endeavor starts with a choice—a conscious decision to venture forth, to take that daring step, to challenge the status quo. By opening this book, you've made that choice. Welcome to Motivate Her, your compass in navigating the vast sea of entrepreneurship.

It's essential to recognize that the mere fact you're here is no small thing. Think of the countless individuals who harbor dreams yet never act on them. Dreams that remain dormant, never given the wings to fly. Yet, here you are, not just dreaming, but seeking. Seeking the knowledge, the guidance, and the tools to bring your vision to life.

Now, let's pose a question: What separates household names in the business realm from ventures that barely see the light of day? The answer isn't merely about financial backing or the right connections, though those can be significant assets. No, the real distinction lies in the interplay of strategy, understanding of human psychology, and an unwavering belief in oneself.

This self-belief isn't born out of arrogance. Instead, it's a profound understanding that within each of us lies a reservoir of untapped potential. The key? Recognizing this potential and giving it the right environment to flourish. Imagine a seed. When placed in fertile soil, given the right amount of water and sunlight, it germinates, grows, and eventually bears fruit. Similarly, your inner business acumen, your 'inner mogul,' if you will, needs the right conditions to truly shine.

But how do we create these conditions? That's where mindset comes into play. If the entrepreneurial journey is a marathon, your mindset is the training you undergo before the race. It's the daily rituals, the beliefs you hold about yourself, and the company you keep. It's the voice inside your head that either says, "This is too hard," or "Let's find a way." Nurturing this voice, steering it towards the latter statement, is foundational.

Throughout this journey, you'll encounter challenges, that's a given. Yet, with the right mindset, these challenges aren't setbacks but opportunities—opportunities to learn, grow, and prove to yourself just how resilient and adaptable you truly are.

Before we delve into actionable strategies and tangible steps to skyrocket your venture, remember this: your greatest asset isn't your bank balance, your connections, or even your business idea. It's you—your beliefs, your drive, and that inner mogul waiting to be unearthed.

GOLDEN PRINCIPLES

So, you're ready to navigate the labyrinth of entrepreneurship, armed with a fortified mindset. Fantastic! But before we embark on this epic odyssey (complete with fewer Cyclopes and more insights on brand building), let's equip you with some golden principles—your business armor, if you will.

1. Value Proposition: Here's a fun thought experiment: If your business were at a party (yes, businesses can party too, in our imagination), how would it introduce itself? Would it blend into the wallpaper, or would it be the life of the soirée? Your value proposition is that introduction. It's the core of what makes you unique and compelling in a market that, let's face it, sometimes feels like it's had a few too many carbon copies.
2. Leverage: Think of leverage as that friend who knows just how to get the best table at a booked-out restaurant or score those concert tickets that were supposedly "sold out." It's all about maximizing your current assets. Whether it's your personal network, resources, or that charm you've been told you have—learning to leverage is like mastering the art of the perfect wink; it gets doors to open.
3. Continuous Learning: Imagine if Sherlock Holmes decided he already knew everything and didn't need to investigate any further. We'd have very short, very boring stories. The business world is your mystery, and it's always evolving. Stay curious, always be in 'investigation mode', and never let your learning cap collect dust.
4. Building Relationships: If business was a movie, relationships would be the leading actor. While profit margins and marketing strategies have their roles, it's relationships that often steal the show. It's not just about having contacts; it's about forming connections. And just like any good film, it's these connections that keep the audience (your clients and partners) engaged.
5. Calculated Risks: Now, we're not suggesting you base your entire business plan on a hunch or the way your tea leaves settled this morning. However, recognizing the right moment to make a move—even if it feels bold or unconventional—is paramount. It's like deciding to wear polka dots with stripes; some might call it audacious, but when done right, it's memorable and groundbreaking.

Imagine, if you will, a garden. Not just any garden, but your business garden. Every enterprise, every brand, every world-altering idea starts as a delicate seed, bursting with potential. However, simply planting that seed won't suffice. Like any proud plant parent would tell you (after proudly showing off photos of their succulent collection), it's the care, commitment, and sometimes the chats with your plants, that truly make the difference.

Now, why am I going on about gardens when this is clearly a business book and not 'Botany 101'? Well, because understanding business growth is a lot like understanding how a garden flourishes. It's an interplay of the right conditions, patience, and learning when to prune and when to nurture.

1. Environment Matters: Just as you wouldn't plant sunflowers in a gloomy corner, your business needs the right environment to thrive. This refers to market conditions, company culture, and even the mental space you create for innovation. You can have the best seed (or idea) in the world, but without the right conditions, its growth will be stunted.

2. Patience is Your Companion: You wouldn't plant a seed today and expect a full-blown tree tomorrow, right? (And if you do, I'd love to see that magical seed supplier of yours.) Similarly, in business, while quick wins are gratifying, building an empire requires patience. It's about recognizing that some things take time and that the journey, with all its twists and turns, offers its own set of invaluable lessons.

3. Adaptability is Key: Ever noticed how plants turn towards the light? That's nature's lesson in adaptability. In the world of business, being rigid is a fast track to obsolescence. It's essential to be receptive to change, to pivot when required, and sometimes, to do the unexpected moonwalk when everyone else is waltzing.

4. Celebrate the Seasons: Every garden has its seasons of bloom and wilt. Similarly, in business, there will be highs and lows. The key is to learn from each phase, to savor the successes and to dissect the downturns. And perhaps, most importantly, to always maintain a sense of humor, because let's face it, sometimes you just have to laugh at the unpredictability of it all.

5. Tend to Your Garden: Neglect a garden, and weeds will overrun it. Neglect your business, and challenges will pile up. Regular check-ins, evaluations, and tweaks will ensure your venture remains on a growth trajectory. Sometimes, this means making tough decisions, and at other times, it's about celebrating milestones with that expensive bottle of bubbly you've been saving.

As we journey deeper into the world of business, this garden analogy will remain pertinent. Just like every gardener has their unique touch, every entrepreneur carves their distinct path. And while I promise not to inundate you with plant metaphors throughout the book, remember this: With the right care, your business garden can transform into a lush, sprawling landscape of success.

Here's to growth, to blossoming, and to the unparalleled joy of watching your vision come to life. Now, grab those metaphorical gardening gloves, and let's get to cultivating your business empire!

CHAPTER 1:
The Female Advantage

At the very core of every groundbreaking venture, beyond the spreadsheets and the conference calls, lies an intrinsic set of qualities—traits that fuel innovation, foster collaboration, and drive exponential growth. As women in the business world, our inherent strengths, forged through centuries of societal roles and life experiences, uniquely position us to not just navigate the complexities of entrepreneurship but to truly thrive within them. So, let's dive into the beautiful tapestry of strengths women bring to the table:

1. Emotional Intelligence (EQ): Recent studies have consistently highlighted that women, on average, tend to have higher emotional intelligence than their male counterparts. This ability to recognize, understand, and manage our emotions—and those of others—isn't just a soft skill. It's a game-changer. From managing teams and leading with empathy to effectively navigating negotiations, a high EQ is akin to having a superpower in the business realm.

2. Collaborative Instinct: Historically, women have often been at the heart of communities, nurturing relationships, and fostering connections.

In business, this translates to a collaborative approach—an intrinsic belief in the "we" over the "me." This mindset promotes teamwork, shared vision, and collective successes, resulting in ventures that are not just profitable but also sustainable.

3. Multitasking Mastery: Though the concept of multitasking has its critics, there's no denying that many women wear numerous hats with seamless grace. Whether juggling parental responsibilities, societal expectations, or managing complex projects, this ability to handle multiple tasks concurrently is an asset. In the ever-evolving world of business, where rapid adaptability is crucial, this skill positions women entrepreneurs a step ahead.

4. Innate Resilience: Let's face it: women have faced, and continue to face, a plethora of challenges—whether societal, professional, or personal. These challenges, though taxing, have also been the crucible within which an extraordinary resilience has been forged. For the female entrepreneur, this resilience isn't just about bouncing back but about growing stronger, more insightful, and even more committed after every setback.

5. Holistic Perspective: Women have an innate ability to view situations holistically. This doesn't just mean looking at the broader picture, but understanding the intricate weave of interconnections within it. In business, this ensures detailed, comprehensive strategies that account for varied outcomes and scenarios, increasing the chances of success.

6. Intuitive Decision Making: While data-driven decisions are paramount in business, there's something to be said about gut instinct—an almost visceral understanding that transcends numbers. Women often possess a keen intuitive sense, honed through a lifetime of experiences, making them adept at making decisions that might seem unconventional but prove to be groundbreaking.

7. Ethical Orientation: Women, in many cultures and societies, have been the moral compasses, instilling values and guiding the next generation. In business, this often translates to an ethical orientation, ensuring that ventures don't just aim for profitability but also contribute positively to society and the environment.

As we venture deeper into this chapter, it's vital to recognize that these qualities aren't about gender binaries or stereotyping. Rather, they're a celebration of the distinct strengths women often bring to the business arena. It's also essential to acknowledge that not every woman will resonate with every trait mentioned. We are, after all, unique individuals with our own set of experiences and skills.

However, understanding these strengths, celebrating them, and harnessing them effectively can be the key to not just succeeding in business but truly revolutionizing it. As we stand on the cusp of a new era of entrepreneurship, it's time to embrace these qualities, amplifying the female advantage and rewriting the rules of the business world. And remember, the most potent blend in business isn't just intellect or strategy—it's the harmonious melding of both with the unique strengths we bring to the table.

Addressing and Debunking Common Misconceptions:

Ah, misconceptions—the unwanted plus-ones of any story of progress. The business realm, particularly when it intersects with womanhood, is not immune to these oft-quoted "truths." But let's face it, many of these are as out of place as a fish riding a bicycle. It's time we not only address these myths but, like a deft magician, debunk them with flair (and perhaps a sprinkle of sass).

1. "Women are too emotional for business."
Oh, where to start? Yes, women may be more in touch with their emotions (thanks, EQ), but that doesn't mean we're on the brink of tears every time the stock market dips. Emotional intelligence is an asset. It enables deeper connections, fosters better team environments, and, let's be honest, sometimes a little empathy goes a long way in sealing the deal.

2. "Women can't handle the pressures of leadership."
Now, this is laughable. Have you ever tried to manage a household with a toddler, a teenager, and a pet—all while holding a full-time job? That's some serious boot camp for handling pressures. Leadership isn't about never facing stress; it's about managing it. And women, through myriad roles, have time and time again proven their mettle.

3. "Businesswomen can't strike a work-life balance."
Here's the thing: the work-life balance challenge isn't exclusive to women. It's a modern-age conundrum that affects everyone. However, with their multitasking prowess, women often have a unique approach to juggling these spheres. Also, can we take a moment to appreciate that maybe, just maybe, not every woman is aspiring for the same kind of balance?

4. "Women-led businesses are cute side hustles, not real ventures."
First off, "cute"? Really? Let's get one thing straight: a business led by a woman is as much a "real" venture as any. Whether it's a tech startup, a fashion line, or a global consultancy—female entrepreneurs are establishing enterprises that are making waves, breaking barriers, and oh yes, making some serious money.

5. "Women are risk-averse in business."
Being calculated and careful doesn't equate to being risk-averse. Women, often, are strategic risk-takers, ensuring that when they take the leap, they've checked the parachute, the weather conditions, and yes, even the view they'll enjoy on the way down.

6. "A woman's business success is often attributed to her looks or connections."
Alright, let's end this charade. While networking and presentation can be assets in the business world, reducing a woman's success to just these factors is not just naive but downright disrespectful. Business acumen, strategy, perseverance, and innovation are often the pillars of their success.

In the evolving narrative of business, these misconceptions might seem like pesky flies—annoying but harmless. However, left unaddressed, they can shape perceptions and limit opportunities. It's imperative to not just recognize these myths for what they are, but to actively challenge and debunk them.

After all, every time we shatter a misconception, we pave the way for a more inclusive, understanding, and ultimately successful business landscape. So, as we forge ahead, let's ensure our journey is guided by facts, experiences, and the undying spirit of entrepreneurship, rather than outdated myths that deserve a rightful place in the annals of history. And between us, let's also enjoy a chuckle or two at their expense.

Harnessing the Power of Female Networks in Business

In the age of connectivity, the saying, "It's not what you know, but who you know" has never been truer. The world, they say, is a vast web of connections, a sprawling network. For women in business, these networks offer a unique strength and source of empowerment, often overlooked but immeasurably valuable.

- Community and Sisterhood: Women have an age-old legacy of forming tight-knit communities, whether it's the village gathering, book clubs, or mommy groups. This instinctive gravitation towards communal connections can be translated into the business world. Female-centric business networks provide not just contacts, but a sense of sisterhood—offering mentorship, guidance, and often, a comforting shoulder during tough times.

- Mentorship Opportunities: Research indicates that women, when in leadership roles, are more likely to mentor other women. This is invaluable. Mentorship provides early-stage entrepreneurs and professionals with guidance, insider knowledge, and, often, opportunities that might be hard to come by otherwise. It's the proverbial passing of the torch, ensuring that the path once trodden becomes easier for those who follow.

- Collaboration Over Competition: While competition is a reality in business, women-led networks often emphasize collaboration. Joint ventures, partnerships, or simply sharing resources—there's a treasure trove of possibilities when women decide to combine forces. It's like joining two pieces of a puzzle; each entity retains its uniqueness but creates something even more substantial together.

- Shared Experiences: One of the most underrated aspects of female networks is the wealth of shared experiences. Whether it's tackling gender biases, managing work-life integration, or dealing with specific industry challenges, there's a collective wisdom in these groups. It's akin to having a massive, ever-evolving playbook that's being written in real-time.

- Economic Empowerment: Female networks often prioritize uplifting each other economically. Whether it's promoting a fellow entrepreneur's product, investing in women-led ventures, or providing platforms for showcasing services—these networks can be powerful economic catalysts.

As we highlight the strengths and advantages women bring to business, recognizing and harnessing the power of female networks becomes paramount. In an ecosystem that's often about cutthroat competition and rapid ascents, these networks remind us of the value of collective growth, shared success, and the magic that unfolds when women uplift women.

The journey of a thousand miles begins with a single step, they say. But when that step is taken alongside a network of like-minded, empowered women, the journey isn't just made more manageable—it becomes an adventure filled with collective victories, and stories that inspire generations to come.

CHAPTER 2:

The Foundation of Your Brand

Ah, passion and purpose. Two words that might sound like the title of a romantic novel, but when applied in the business context, they become the very core of any successful brand. They're the kindling that ignites the flame, the wind beneath the wings of every groundbreaking idea. Let's navigate this, shall we?

1. Introspection is Key

First, take a moment, sit back, perhaps with a cup of your favorite beverage (mine's a latte with an extra shot, in case you're wondering). Reflect on those moments when you felt most alive. What activities engross you so much that you lose track of time? Whether it's crafting intricate jewelry, designing software solutions, or baking the fluffiest of pastries—there lies a clue.

2. Remember Childhood Dreams

Sometimes, our younger selves knew better. Remember when you were ten and wanted to rule the world or at least a candy store? Those dreams, while they may have evolved, still have kernels of your intrinsic passions. There's genuine wisdom in revisiting them, filtering them through your adult experiences and skills.

3. The Intersection of Skills and Joy

Your passion often resides where what you're good at overlaps with what brings you joy. It's like the sweet spot in a Venn diagram. If you're a numbers whiz and find absolute ecstasy in helping others manage their finances, voila, you might be looking at a financial consultancy venture!

4. Purpose is Bigger Than Profit

While it's lovely (and necessary) for businesses to turn a profit, a brand built solely around money often lacks depth. Your purpose is your north star, guiding every decision, big or small. Whether it's sustainability, empowering local artisans, or offering unmatched quality—your purpose gives your brand its soul.

5. Seek Feedback

Sometimes, we're too close to the canvas to see the bigger picture. Ask friends, family, or mentors what they think you're passionate about. Often, they'll offer insights you might have overlooked. Just a heads-up: Be prepared for some unexpected revelations!

6. The Passion-Purpose Litmus Test

This is simple. If you were to win the lottery tomorrow (fingers crossed), would you still want to pursue this activity even if money wasn't a factor? If the answer is a resounding yes, you've probably hit the jackpot in the passion department.

7. Evolution is Natural

As humans, we evolve, and so do our passions and purposes. It's okay if what fired you up five years ago doesn't quite do it anymore. The key is continuous introspection and alignment. After all, your brand should be a reflection of your authentic self.

8. Marry Passion with Market Need

Lastly, while passion and purpose are crucial, ensure there's a market need for your offering. Your passion might be crafting unicorn-shaped marzipan candies (and honestly, who wouldn't love that?), but is there a substantial audience out there for it? A little market research goes a long way.

Discovering your passion and purpose is akin to an archaeological dig, unearthing treasures that have always been there, just waiting to shine. They become the bedrock of your brand, infusing authenticity and enthusiasm in every facet. It's like magnetism, really. When you radiate passion, your audience, your clients, your market—they all gravitate towards you. And that, my friend, is the genesis of a million-dollar brand.

7 DAYS TO FINDING YOUR PASSION & PURPOSE

- Day 1: Memory Lane Dive

Task: Take out some old photo albums, journals, or even your childhood toys. Dive deep into memories of when you were joyful, proud, or super engaged.

Journal Prompt: Write about three activities from your childhood that made you lose track of time.

- Day 2: The Compliment Collector

Task: Reach out to at least five close friends or family members. Ask them, "What do you think I'm exceptionally good at?"

Journal Prompt: Note down the recurring themes or surprises from the feedback received.

- Day 3: The 'No Money Involved' Fantasy

Task: Imagine you've won an all-expenses-paid life. Money's no object anymore. What would you spend your days doing?

Journal Prompt: Describe your ideal day in this fantasy. From the moment you wake up to when you go to bed. What activities stand out?

- Day 4: The Skills and Joys Overlap

Task: Make two lists. On one, jot down things you're good at. On the other, things that bring you immense joy. Where do the lists overlap?

Journal Prompt: Reflect on the overlapping items. Do any of them surprise you? Can you see a business idea forming?

- Day 5: The Market Researcher

Task: Take one of the overlapping items from Day 4. Do a quick market analysis. Who else is doing it? What's the demand?

Journal Prompt: Document your findings. Is there a niche you could fill? Is there a unique twist you can bring to the table?

- Day 6: The Dream Vision Board

Task: Create a vision board. This can be digital or physical. Fill it with images, quotes, and anything else that resonates with your discovered passion and purpose.

Journal Prompt: How does your vision board make you feel? What dreams or goals surface as you look at it?

- Day 7: Reflection and Commitment

Task: Sit in a quiet space. Reflect on the week gone by. What revelations stood out?

Journal Prompt: Write a commitment letter to yourself. What steps will you take next, now that you've honed in on your passion and purpose? Set clear, actionable goals.

There you have it—a week-long challenge designed to not only help you rediscover yourself but also to lay the foundational stone for your brand. Remember, passion and purpose are like the roots of a tree. The deeper they go, the taller and stronger the tree stands.

Now let's dive into building your vision and mission statement.

Vision and mission statements are, quite simply, the heartbeat of your brand. They provide direction, drive decisions, and define the very core of why your brand exists. They're more than just catchy phrases on a website or a business card. They're the guiding lights that steer your venture towards its purpose, anchoring it amidst the storms and uncertainties of the business world.

1. The Vision Statement: The Distant Horizon

Think of your vision statement as the distant horizon—the ultimate goal you're steering towards. It's the "where we want to be" of your brand. It's ambitious, forward-looking, and paints a picture of the brand's long-term aspirations.

Tip: Make it aspirational. Your vision statement should feel slightly out of reach; it's a reflection of the heights you aim to achieve.

2. The Mission Statement: The Route to That Horizon

While the vision is the destination, the mission is the path. It answers the question, "How will we get there?" It outlines the purpose of your business, its primary functions, and its target audience.

Tip: Make it actionable. This isn't just about lofty goals; it's about the concrete steps you'll take to reach that distant horizon.

3. Reflect on Your Brand's Core

Before penning down these statements, dive deep into the ethos of your brand. What are its core values? Who are its stakeholders? What change do you aim to drive in the world with your product or service?

4. Keep it Concise

While it's tempting to craft a sweeping narrative, brevity is key. Your vision and mission should be punchy, memorable, and easy to recall. Think of them as your brand's elevator pitch to the world.

5. Involve Your Team

If you have a team or trusted confidants, involve them in the process. Sometimes, diverse perspectives can crystallize thoughts and ideas that might be nebulous in your head.

6. Iterate and Evolve

Your vision and mission statements aren't set in stone. As your brand grows, and as you grow with it, allow these statements the flexibility to evolve. They should mirror the dynamic nature of your business and the market it operates in.

7. Make it Visible

Once crafted, let these statements be the torchbearers of your brand identity. Incorporate them into your brand collateral, your website, your office space—everywhere. They should serve as daily reminders of why you started and where you're headed.

Crafting a vision and mission statement might seem like a daunting task. Still, it's essentially a reflection of your brand's soul, encapsulated in a few succinct lines. So take a deep breath, reflect on what drives you and your brand, and start charting out that brilliant path forward. After all, every significant journey begins with clarity of purpose and destination.

MISSION STATEMENT EXAMPLES

1. Technology: "Our mission is to empower every individual and every organization on the planet to achieve more."

2. Health and Fitness: "We exist to inspire and enable every person to unlock their inner athlete and harness the limitless power of their body and mind."

3. Fashion: "To reimagine the fabric of fashion by blending timeless designs with sustainable practices, creating a world where style meets responsibility."

4. Education: "Championing lifelong learning by making world-class educational resources accessible to all, bridging gaps and fostering global citizens."

5. Food and Beverage: "Crafting delightful culinary experiences by harnessing the purity of natural ingredients, bringing families closer one meal at a time."

6. Non-Profit (Environmental): "To safeguard our planet's future by championing sustainable practices, fostering a global community of eco-warriors, and nurturing nature's regenerative power."

7. Travel and Hospitality: "We venture to craft unforgettable journeys, weaving local cultures and untold stories, helping travelers not just visit, but belong."

8. E-Commerce: "Bringing the world's marketplace to your doorstep – where quality meets convenience, and every purchase tells a story."

9. Arts and Entertainment: "Celebrating the human spirit through art, creating platforms where stories come alive, cultures converge, and creativity knows no bounds."

10. Personal Coaching: "To ignite the flames of potential in every soul I encounter, guiding them on a journey of self-discovery, growth, and boundless success."

11. Real Estate: "Transforming landscapes and lives, one property at a time. We are committed to creating spaces where memories are made, dreams are realized, and every square foot tells a story of home."

When crafting your mission statement, it's crucial to ensure it's authentic to your brand's core values and ethos. Let these examples inspire you, but remember, your unique mission will resonate most powerfully when it's a true reflection of your brand's essence and vision.

Brand Differentiation and USP (Unique Selling Proposition)

In the cacophonous marketplace of the modern world, where every brand is vying for attention, standing out isn't just an advantage—it's a necessity. The keystone of memorable branding? Differentiation and a rock-solid USP.

1. Understanding Brand Differentiation

Branding isn't about slapping a logo on your product or getting a catchy jingle. It's the promise you make to your customers. Brand differentiation is the method by which that promise is made unique.

Key Takeaway: It's not always about being better; sometimes, it's about being different in a way that matters to your target audience.

2. The Essence of a Unique Selling Proposition (USP)

Your USP is the singular reason consumers should choose you over competitors. It's a blend of what you do differently and why that difference is valuable.

Key Takeaway: Your USP doesn't need to appeal to everyone, but it should resonate deeply with your ideal client or customer.

3. Dig Deep: The 'Why' Before the 'What'

Before you pinpoint what makes your brand different, understand why you started your venture. Your personal "why" can often lead to your brand's most potent differentiator.

Task: Reflect on your origins, your motivations, and the problem you set out to solve. Often, within those narratives lies your differentiator.

4. Evaluating the Market Landscape

Understanding what's out there is pivotal. Study your competitors, not to imitate them, but to understand where there's a gap, an unmet need, or a unique twist you can introduce.

Key Takeaway: In real estate, the mantra is location, location, location. In branding? It's differentiation, differentiation, differentiation.

5. Tangible vs. Intangible Differentiators

Your differentiator can be something tangible—like a patented technology—or intangible, like a brand story that resonates or unparalleled customer service.

Activity: List down five tangible and five intangible assets of your brand. See which ones truly set you apart.

6. Crafting Your USP Statement

Once you've pinned down your differentiators, weave them into a compelling USP statement. It should be concise, memorable, and instantly communicate your brand's unique value.

Tip: Test your USP on a small group. Does it resonate? Is it clear and compelling? Use feedback to refine it.

7. Living Your Differentiator

Your differentiator and USP aren't just for marketing collateral. They should permeate every aspect of your business, from operations to customer interactions.

Key Takeaway: Authenticity is key. If you claim a differentiator, ensure every touchpoint with your brand reinforces it.

8. Continuous Evolution

The market isn't static, and neither should your brand be. Regularly revisit and reassess your differentiators and USP to ensure they remain relevant and compelling.

Task: Schedule bi-annual brand audits to assess how well you're living up to your USP and where adjustments might be needed.

In real estate, properties might seem similar: a set number of bedrooms, a particular square footage. But it's the little things—the view from the balcony, the neighborhood's charm, the memories made within those walls—that set one property apart from another. Similarly, in business, the nuances, the stories, the values, and the promises make all the difference.

Emotional Branding: Where Heart Meets Business

Imagine for a moment you're perusing a store shelf or scrolling online, and a brand sparks a familiar warmth, like meeting an old friend. It's more than just a logo or a catchy slogan; it's a feeling, an emotional resonance. That, dear reader, is the power of emotional branding.

At the core of our decisions, no matter how logical we like to think we are, emotions reign supreme. This isn't a soft fact; it's hardwired into our psychology. When a brand makes us feel seen, understood, or part of a bigger narrative, we don't just become customers; we transform into loyalists, advocates—even brand evangelists.

Now, let's talk stories. Not fairy tales, but the journey of your brand, the dreams, hurdles, moments of euphoria, and even the occasional stumbles. This narrative is gold. It's what differentiates a faceless corporation from a brand with heart and soul. So, dive into your history, unearth those moments, and share them with the world.

But here's a little secret: Consistency is your magic wand. It's one thing to make someone feel a burst of emotion once, but to do it time and again, across every interaction and platform? That's what dreams (and successful brands) are made of. So, as you venture into the vast realms of digital marketing, social media, or even traditional channels, keep that emotional undertone consistent. It's like the comforting chorus of a song, familiar and heartwarming.

In the end, remember, the most iconic brands, the ones etched in the annals of business history, went beyond selling a product. They sold a feeling. In this age of information overload and endless choices, standing out is about making your audience feel. Feel recognized, cherished, and part of your brand's story.

So, here's your mantra for the day: Logic may catch attention, but emotions? They capture hearts. And that's where true brand loyalty is born.

Let's take a look at a few brands whose mission statements and USPs (Unique Selling Propositions) have significantly aided their positioning in the market.

- Nike
    - Mission Statement: "To bring inspiration and innovation to every athlete in the world."
    - USP: Nike's renowned "Just Do It" slogan emphasizes empowerment and determination. The brand stands out by promoting athleticism and perseverance.
- Slack
    - Mission Statement: "To make work life simpler, more pleasant, and more productive."
    - USP: Unlike other communication tools, Slack positions itself as more than just a messaging app—it's a hub for team collaboration and productivity.
- Warby Parker
    - Mission Statement: "To offer designer eyewear at a revolutionary price, while leading the way for socially conscious businesses."
    - USP: Not only does Warby Parker offer affordable, stylish eyewear, but for every pair of glasses sold, a pair is distributed to someone in need.
- Airbnb
    - Mission Statement: "To help create a world where you can belong anywhere."
    - USP: Instead of just being another hotel booking site, Airbnb promotes unique travel experiences by allowing people to stay in real homes and feel like locals.
- Tesla
    - Mission Statement: "To accelerate the world's transition to sustainable energy."
    - USP: While there are many car manufacturers, Tesla's commitment to electric vehicles, cutting-edge

technology, and sustainability sets it apart from traditional automakers.
- TOMS
    - Mission Statement: "We're in business to improve lives."
    - USP: For every product you purchase, TOMS will help someone in need through their 'One for One' promise.
- Lush Cosmetics
    - Mission Statement: "To make fresh, natural products that do good for the hair, skin, and environment."
    - USP: Lush emphasizes hand-made, cruelty-free, and environmentally-friendly beauty products, carving out a unique niche in the cosmetics industry.

These brands have succeeded not just because of superior products or services, but because they've connected with consumers on a deeper, value-based level. Their mission statements and USPs aren't just about what they do but why they do it, making consumers feel good about their choices.

CHAPTER 3:
Brand Aesthetics and Identity

The realm of business is vast, saturated, and at times, relentless. Amongst this intense competition, what makes one brand stand out while another fades into the shadows? More often than not, it's not just the product or service but the aesthetics and identity of the brand. Let's uncover why a cohesive look and feel isn't just a superficial decision, but a strategic one.

1. Immediate Recognition

Imagine walking through a crowded marketplace. Your eyes wander from stall to stall, but then you spot that signature Tiffany blue or the unmistakable 'swoosh' of Nike. These brands have become so entrenched in our minds that we can spot them from miles away. That's the power of cohesive branding. A consistent aesthetic allows for immediate recognition, which in turn prompts recall of positive associations with the brand.

2. Trust Building

Consistency breeds trust. When consumers encounter the same visuals, messaging, and tone every time they interact with a brand, they feel a sense of familiarity. This familiarity, over time, translates into trust. It sends a message: "We know who we are, and we're confident in our promise to you."

3. Emotional Resonance

We humans are visual creatures. We're drawn to beauty, to symmetry, to patterns we recognize. A well-thought-out and consistent brand aesthetic can evoke emotions — tranquility, excitement, nostalgia, or aspiration. This isn't about duping your audience but about connecting with them on a deeper, emotional level. When people feel, they remember.

4. Differentiation in the Market

In a sea of sameness, it's the distinct fish that gets noticed. With industries overflowing with similar products, what makes one choose brand A over brand B? It's the distinct identity. A brand that invests in a unique look and feel sets itself apart, offering something visually fresh and enticing to its audience.

5. Enhances Brand Value

A cohesive brand aesthetic is a sign of professionalism. It indicates that the company invests in its image and takes its brand seriously. This perceived value can often allow brands to charge a premium for their products or services. It's not just about what you offer but how you present what you offer.

6. Fosters Brand Loyalty

Loyalty isn't just about how good your product is. It's about how your brand makes people feel.

When consumers identify with your brand's aesthetics and values, they're more likely to stay loyal. They wear your brand, use your product, or engage with your service as a badge of personal identity.

Practical Steps for Building a Cohesive Brand Aesthetic:

- Research: Before you decide on colors, logos, or typefaces, research your target demographic. What appeals to them? What visuals resonate with their lifestyle, aspirations, and needs?
- Consistency is Key: Choose a color palette, typeface, and logo that reflects your brand's core values and stick with them. This doesn't mean you can't evolve, but drastic changes can alienate your existing consumer base.
- Tell a Story: Every element of your brand, from the color palette to the images used, should tell your brand's story. Are you a sustainable brand promoting an eco-friendly lifestyle? Nature-inspired colors and imagery might be your go-to.
- Quality Over Quantity: Invest in high-quality visuals. Whether it's product photography, website design, or promotional materials, the quality of your visuals speaks volumes about the quality of your brand.
- Seek Feedback: Regularly check in with your audience. Does your aesthetic resonate with them? Are there elements they love or dislike?

A brand's aesthetic is much more than just a "pretty face." It's the first impression, the lasting memory, and the silent ambassador of your brand. In a world where every swipe, click, or scroll introduces us to a new brand, ensure yours stands out, not just for what it offers, but for the captivating story it tells visually.

Understanding the Subtleties of Brand Aesthetics and Identity

When we talk about brand aesthetics and identity, it's easy to get caught up in the visual elements: logos, color palettes, and typography. While these are undoubtedly crucial, it's essential to delve deeper into the nuances that subtly influence a brand's perception.

Emotion Through Design

Every design choice made for a brand evokes emotion. Take color, for instance. Blue might represent trust and dependability, often used by financial institutions, while a vibrant orange might give off energy and enthusiasm, commonly associated with fitness or youth-centered brands. It's not just about selecting a color you "like" but choosing one that conveys the emotions and attributes you want associated with your business.

Sensory Touchpoints

While the visual element of a brand is paramount, especially in the digital age, other sensory touchpoints shouldn't be ignored. The texture of a product's packaging, the sound of an ad's jingle, or the scent released when entering a store all contribute to brand identity. Apple's product design, from the feel of the MacBook's aluminum case to the smoothness of an iPhone screen, exemplifies sensory branding in action.

Consistency vs. Adaptability

Consistency in brand aesthetics solidifies recognition, but adaptability ensures a brand remains relevant.

It's a delicate balance. Brands might undergo design "refreshes" over the years, subtly updating logos or changing color gradients slightly. These changes can be so discreet that customers might not immediately notice, but they're vital in ensuring a brand feels contemporary.

Narrative Through Imagery

The photos and graphics a brand uses tell a story. It's more than just showcasing a product; it's about conveying an experience or lifestyle. The images chosen should resonate with the target audience's aspirations, desires, or needs. For example, a luxury brand may use photos of models in exotic locations or lavish settings, conveying a narrative of exclusivity and opulence.

Integration Across Platforms

Today's brands exist in a myriad of spaces - both physical and digital. It's essential that the brand identity is flexible enough to be translated across various platforms without losing its essence. This might mean that while the color palette remains consistent, the way it's presented might change slightly from a Facebook cover photo to a billboard advertisement.

Interactive Exercise: "The Brand Mood Board Challenge"

Objective:

Create a mood board that visually represents your brand's aesthetic and identity. This is a fun, interactive way to see if what you've envisioned for your brand resonates when placed side by side.

Materials Needed:

- A large poster board or digital platform (like Pinterest, Canva, or Adobe Spark).
- Magazines, printouts, color swatches, or digital images.
- Scissors and glue (for physical mood boards).
- Notes or captions (for digital mood boards).

Steps:

1. Define Your Brand in Three Words:
    - Write down three words that best describe your brand. Examples: Fresh, Professional, Adventurous; Chic, Sustainable, Bold.

2. Gather Inspirational Images:
    - Physically: Flip through magazines, printouts, or color swatches and cut out images, colors, and words that resonate with your brand's three defining words.
    - Digitally: Search for images, color palettes, and typography that align with your brand's feel. Save them to a specific folder or pin them to your board.

3. Organize & Arrange:
    - Place your images, colors, and words on the board without gluing or finalizing. Play with arrangements.
    - Digitally, drag and arrange images and elements to create a cohesive look.

4. Reflect & Adjust:
    - Step back and look at your mood board. Does it resonate with your brand's three words? Is there a flow? Does it feel like 'you' or 'your brand'?
    - Make adjustments, remove or add elements as you see fit.

5. Finalize Your Mood Board:
    - Physically: Once satisfied, glue everything down.
    - Digitally: Finalize the layout, add any text or captions if needed, and save.

6. Share & Seek Feedback:
    - If possible, share your mood board with someone else. Ask them what three words come to mind when they see it. Do their words align with yours?
    - Take their feedback with an open mind. Adjust if necessary.

7. Apply & Integrate:
    - Use your mood board as a reference when making decisions about your brand aesthetic. Whether it's your website design, social media post, or product packaging, refer back to your mood board for inspiration and guidance.

Remember, a mood board is not set in stone. As your brand grows and evolves, feel free to create a new board.

Symbols in Branding

Symbols have been a foundational aspect of human communication since the dawn of civilization. From cave paintings to hieroglyphics, they've played an integral role in conveying ideas, emotions, and stories. In the realm of branding, symbols serve as a bridge between the tangible and the intangible, capturing the essence of a brand's identity and its promise to the consumer in a concise visual format.

Consider the Nike Swoosh, Apple's iconic apple, or the golden arches of McDonald's. Without uttering a single word, these symbols evoke a realm of emotions, associations, and expectations. They transcend languages, cultures, and demographics, allowing for global recognition. In a split second, a well-designed symbol can tell you what a brand stands for, what it promises, and why you should care.

- Instantaneous Emotional Connection: When someone sees a brand's symbol, the brain instantly processes it, linking to prior experiences, emotions, and perceptions related to that brand. If your brand symbol resonates with positivity and trust, consumers are more likely to gravitate towards your offerings.
- Versatility in Application: Symbols are incredibly flexible. They can be used in a multitude of scenarios, from the tiniest social media icon to a massive billboard. Their scalable nature ensures brand consistency across various mediums.
- Memorable & Timeless: A great symbol has longevity. While certain branding elements might need periodic updates, a strong, timeless symbol can endure changes in market trends and shifts in company strategy.

- Universal Communication: In an increasingly globalized market, symbols can bridge communication gaps. They transcend linguistic barriers, ensuring that your brand's essence is universally understood.

So, how do you go about choosing the right symbol for your brand? Begin by understanding the core values and messages you want to convey. Dive deep into the psyche of your target audience: What resonates with them? What emotions do you wish to evoke? Once you're clear on these aspects, collaborate with skilled designers who can transform these intangible ideas into a visual masterpiece.

Always ensure that your chosen symbol is unique, preventing potential confusion with other brands and ensuring that you stand out in a saturated market. When executed right, a brand's symbol becomes its silent ambassador, making powerful impressions long before words ever come into play.

Typography Matters: The Psychology of Fonts

Typography – the unsung hero of the branding universe. It's more than just letters on a screen or paper; it's an embodiment of your brand's voice, character, and soul. Think of typography as that friend with an impeccable dress sense: just the right attire for every occasion, always making an impression without saying a word.

So, why does typography hold such sway in the grand scheme of branding?

- It Evokes Emotion: Just like how different colors can ignite distinct feelings, fonts have their own emotional resonance.

Serif fonts, with their classic tiny feet or 'serifs,' have a timeless, reliable, and authoritative feel. Think The New York Times. On the flip side, sans-serif fonts, without these 'feet,' offer a modern, clean, and no-nonsense vibe, which you'll often find on tech companies' sites.

- Sets Tone and Voice: If your brand was a person, what would it sound like? A formal butler or a vivacious party planner? The typography you choose sets the tonal stage for this imagined voice. A quirky font might be great for a children's toy store but could seem out of place for a law firm.

- Enhances Readability: Beyond aesthetics, typography's main job is to ensure legibility. You could have the most compelling content in the world, but if your audience can't comfortably read it, what's the point? The balance between style and substance is essential.

- Reinforces Brand Consistency: Consistent typography across all branding materials and platforms solidifies your brand identity. It makes your brand instantly recognizable, be it on a billboard, your website, or a product label.

Now, diving into the nitty-gritty, the science behind it is equally riveting. Studies suggest that fonts can influence a reader's perception of the content. For instance, a study found that readers were more likely to agree with a statement written in a clear, easy-to-read font than one written in a complicated, challenging-to-read style. It all ties back to cognitive ease; our brains prefer things that are easy to process.

Adapting to Different Mediums

Imagine you're at a cocktail party. When introducing yourself to someone across a small table, you'd likely lean in and speak in soft, cordial tones. Later, when announcing a toast to a large audience, your voice would naturally rise in both volume and energy. The message is the same, but the delivery is adapted based on the environment. This, in essence, is the art and science of adapting your brand across various mediums.

- Know Your Medium: Each platform, from the tiny canvas of a business card to the vast expanse of a billboard, has its own set of rules. For instance, while a detailed logo might look stunning on your website or storefront, it might lose its charm when shrunk down to fit on a pen or keychain. Likewise, a message that has a significant impact on a billboard, given its size and the speed at which viewers typically pass by, needs to be short, bold, and instantly graspable.

- Consistency is Key: Regardless of size or platform, your brand's core elements — colors, typography, logos — should remain consistent. This doesn't mean they can't be tweaked or adjusted based on the medium, but they should always be instantly identifiable as "you."

- Master the Art of Scaling: Effective scaling isn't just about making things bigger or smaller. It's about understanding the nuances of each medium. A business card offers an intimate, tactile experience, allowing for finer details and textures. Meanwhile, billboards require bold, clear visuals and text to catch a passerby's attention. Learn to play to each medium's strengths.

- Digital vs. Print: In our digital age, it's crucial to recognize that colors, designs, and fonts might appear differently on screen compared to when they're printed. Always test and adjust your branding materials to ensure they shine both online and offline.

- Feedback Loop: Regularly gather feedback on how your brand appears across different platforms. Just because it looks good on a design mock-up doesn't mean it translates well in real-world applications. Continuous feedback allows for adjustments and fine-tuning.

- Stay Updated: As technology and design trends evolve, so should the way your brand adapts to various mediums. The emergence of augmented reality (AR) and virtual reality (VR) platforms, for example, offers innovative ways to present your brand.

Remember, your brand is more than a logo or a catchy slogan; it's an experience. And each medium offers a unique opportunity to tailor this experience for your audience. Adapting isn't about losing your brand's essence, but about amplifying its core in ways that resonate, no matter where it's encountered.

Brand Aesthetics and Identity Checklist

Brand Analysis
- [] Define your brand's core values.
- [] Identify your target audience and their preferences.
- [] Review competitor brands' aesthetics – what do you like, and what do you want to differentiate from?

Visual Identity
- [] Choose a primary color palette (2-4 colors) that reflects your brand's personality.
- [] Decide on secondary or accent colors (if necessary).
- [] Select a consistent typeface for headers, sub-headers, and body text.
- [] Design a logo that's versatile (works in color and black & white, scalable for different platforms).
- [] Ensure all visuals align with the brand's story and values.

Content Consistency
- [] Use consistent filters or photo-editing styles for images.
- [] Develop a recognizable tone of voice for written content.
- [] Ensure content themes align with brand values and audience interests.

Digital Presence
- [] Design or update your website to reflect the chosen aesthetics.
- [] Ensure social media profiles are consistent with the brand look and feel.
- [] Check that email templates (newsletters, promotional emails) are in line with brand aesthetics.

Printed Materials
- [] Update business cards, brochures, and other printed materials to match your brand identity.
- [] Ensure product packaging (if applicable) aligns with brand aesthetics.

Feedback & Evolution
- [] Seek feedback from stakeholders, loyal customers, or a focus group.
- [] Regularly review and refresh visuals to keep the brand relevant but maintain core aesthetics.
- [] Stay updated with design trends to ensure the brand doesn't appear outdated.

Consistency Audit
- [] Periodically, take a step back and view all brand materials together. Does everything look like it belongs to the same brand?
- [] Make adjustments where needed to ensure cohesion.

Story Alignment
- [] Does every visual and piece of content tell or contribute to your brand's story?
- [] If not, consider adjustments to more closely align with your brand narrative.

Remember, while this checklist is extensive, the essence of brand aesthetics and identity revolves around consistency, alignment with values, and genuine connection with your target audience. Always be open to growth and evolution, but let it be guided by the brand's foundational principles.

BRAND CASE STUDIES

In the sprawling world of branding, a few trailblazers have not just followed the rules but defined them. Here's a look at some brands that have set the gold standard for aesthetics and branding, teaching us invaluable lessons along the way.

1. Magnolia (Joanna Gaines): Beyond being a home renovation celebrity alongside her husband on "Fixer Upper", Joanna Gaines built Magnolia into a lifestyle brand. With its clean, rustic, and homey aesthetic, Magnolia stands out as a beacon of warm minimalism. From home goods to books, every product echoes Joanna's personal style and commitment to family and home.
Lesson: Authenticity in branding attracts a loyal audience. Your genuine passions can guide your brand's aesthetic.

2. Glossier (Emily Weiss): Beginning as a beauty blog called "Into The Gloss", Glossier transformed into a cosmetics juggernaut by focusing on real women and their real beauty routines. Its minimalist packaging and focus on natural beauty have set it apart in the crowded beauty market.
Lesson: Listen to your audience. Understanding and catering to their needs can lead to brand loyalty.

3. Spanx (Sara Blakely): Sara identified a gap in the market and filled it ingeniously with Spanx. Its branding has always been about empowerment, confidence, and embracing one's body. The brand's aesthetic is functional yet feminine, aligning perfectly with its mission.
Lesson: Identify a gap in the market and brand your solution in a way that emotionally resonates with potential users.

4. Nasty Gal (Sophia Amoruso): Starting as an eBay store selling vintage clothes, Nasty Gal grew into a multi-million-dollar brand. Though it faced its challenges, its edgy and fearless branding resonated with young women globally.
Lesson: Be bold. An unapologetic brand voice can help you stand out and resonate with a specific audience.

5. The Honest Company (Jessica Alba): Stemming from a personal need for safe and effective baby products, Jessica Alba's Honest Company is all about transparency and trust. Its clean and calm branding aligns with its promise of natural, safe products.
Lesson: Transparency builds trust. When your brand stands for a cause or value, make it evident in every aspect of your branding.

6. Rifle Paper Co. (Anna Bond): Known for its hand-painted illustrations, this stationery and lifestyle brand brings beauty to everyday items. Their intricate, colorful designs have made them stand out in a digital age, proving there's still a place for traditional artistry.
Lesson: Embrace your unique skills. A distinctive aesthetic or approach can set you apart in a saturated market.

Each of these brands, while different in their offerings, carries a clear and strong aesthetic. These women entrepreneurs have demonstrated that with clarity of vision, understanding of their audience, and a commitment to authenticity, brands can achieve success and resonate deeply with consumers.

CHAPTER 4:
Marketing & Branding Psychology

Marketing isn't just about splashing your brand on every billboard or pushing ads at every corner of the internet. At its core, marketing is a deeply psychological endeavor. It's about understanding what makes us tick, why we make certain choices, and how emotions sway our decisions. Let's peel back the layers of human psyche and see what drives our behaviors in the marketplace.

Emotion: The Unseen Hand Behind Every Purchase

Delve deep into why we buy, and it's almost never about the logical features of a product. We buy experiences, feelings, and the promise of a particular emotion. Think about it:

- A luxury car is not just about transport; it's the feeling of prestige and class.
- Skincare isn't just about hydration; it's the promise of feeling youthful and radiant.

Brands that understand and leverage this truth can create powerful narratives that make their products irresistible.

Understanding Justification: The "Why" Behind Every Choice

We're rational creatures – at least, we like to think so. But even in our most impulsive purchases, there's an underlying need to justify our actions. Successful marketers anticipate this. They provide consumers with reasons, creating narratives that align with their personal values or aspirations. So, the next time you see a product highlighting its eco-friendliness, it's not just about being green – it's about resonating with the conscious consumer's values and giving them a justifiable reason to choose that product.

The Tug of Reciprocity

Humans have an innate desire to repay kindness. It's why free webinars, e-books, or samples are such powerful marketing tools. They tap into the principle of reciprocity. When we receive something for free, there's an unconscious urge to return the favor. Marketers who master this delicate balance – offering genuine value without overtly expecting something in return – can forge deeper, more meaningful relationships with their customers.

The Social Game: Riding the Wave of FOMO and Social Proof

While we cherish our individuality, there's a tribal element to human behavior. We're influenced by what others are doing. We often seek validation from our peers. This dual phenomenon of the Fear of Missing Out (FOMO) and the power of social proof is why:

- Limited edition drops have people queuing for hours.

- Bestseller tags can significantly boost a book's sales.
- Testimonials can make or break a product.

By acknowledging the deep-seated human need to be part of a group, marketers can create campaigns that foster community and belonging.

Bringing It All Together

Every time we, as consumers, engage with a brand or product, there's an intricate psychological ballet playing out beneath the surface. For the astute marketer, understanding these nuances is the key to crafting campaigns that don't just sell but resonate. It's about reaching out, connecting, and creating shared stories and experiences. And for the empowered women entrepreneurs reading this: by fusing this understanding of human psychology with the unique perspective you bring, the sky's the limit. So, let's dive deeper, understand more, and create marketing magic.

Cognitive Biases: The Invisible Strings Guiding Consumers

Whenever we face decisions, our brains, always on the lookout for shortcuts, rely on cognitive biases. These biases are not flaws per se, but ingrained mechanisms honed over millennia to help us process vast amounts of information quickly. They're like the auto-pilot mode of our cognitive system. For marketers, understanding these biases isn't about manipulation, but about better aligning with how consumers naturally think and feel.

1. Confirmation Bias: Seeing What We Want to See
This is the tendency for people to seek out and interpret

information in a way that confirms their pre-existing beliefs. For instance, if someone believes a particular skincare brand is the best, they might only notice positive reviews about it and ignore the negative ones.

Marketing Play: Brands should create content that resonates with the beliefs and values of their target audience. Offering testimonials or positive reviews can reinforce these beliefs.

2. Anchoring Bias: The Power of the First Impression
The first piece of information we come across (the anchor) tends to have an outsized influence on our subsequent decisions. This is why the initial price shown before a discount can make the discounted price seem like a fantastic deal.

Marketing Play: By presenting the original price before showcasing a sale, brands can make consumers feel they're getting exceptional value.

3. The Bandwagon Effect: Everyone's Doing It
As social beings, we often look to others to guide our decisions, especially in ambiguous situations. If a lot of people are buying or endorsing a product, we're more likely to do the same.
Marketing Play: Showcase user-generated content, testimonials, or the number of products sold to harness this effect.

4. The Scarcity Bias: Fear of Missing Out
We're wired to value things that are scarce more than those that are abundant. Limited-time offers or products running out of stock can trigger this bias, making consumers more inclined to make impulsive purchases.

Marketing Play: Use phrases like "limited stock," "only a few left," or "sale ends soon" to instill a sense of urgency.

5. Loss Aversion: We Hate Losing
People tend to prefer avoiding losses over acquiring equivalent gains. The pain of losing $10 is more intense than the pleasure of gaining the same amount.
Marketing Play: Brands can highlight what consumers might lose out on, rather than just the benefits. For instance, "Don't miss out on glowing skin this winter" can be more compelling than "Get glowing skin this winter."

6. The Halo Effect: One Good Thing Leads to Another
When we see a person or brand excel in one area, we tend to assume they're excellent in other areas as well. A brand known for excellent customer service might also be perceived as having high-quality products.
Marketing Play: By cultivating excellence or goodwill in one domain (like corporate social responsibility), brands can create positive associations in other areas.

7. Status Quo Bias: Better the Devil You Know
People generally prefer keeping things the same. We're resistant to change, even if that change might be beneficial.
Marketing Play: Brands trying to lure customers from competitors need to not only highlight their product's advantages but also mitigate any perceived risks of switching.

Cognitive biases shape the intricate dance between consumers and brands. By understanding these biases, marketers can craft strategies that resonate more deeply, connect more authentically, and deliver messages that align with the very heart of human decision-making. For our readers, especially women entrepreneurs with their unique perspectives, leveraging these insights can be the game-changer in creating campaigns that genuinely move and motivate.

Colors and Their Meanings

Colors aren't just shades on a spectrum; they're silent storytellers, encapsulating millennia of human emotions, experiences, and cultural interpretations. From the fiery red of a passionate heart to the calming blue of a serene sea, colors carry with them an emotional weight that can deeply impact our perceptions and behaviors. For businesses, particularly in branding and marketing, understanding the psychological underpinnings of colors can become the secret ingredient to forging more profound connections with customers.

1. Red: Passion, Energy, Urgency Red is fiery, bold, and demands attention. Think of stop signs, clearance sales, and Valentine's Day. It evokes emotions of love, passion, danger, or even anger. In the world of marketing, it's often used to elicit urgency or to make a bold statement.

2. Blue: Trust, Calm, Dependability There's a reason why many corporate logos, especially in the finance sector, are blue. Blue exudes trust, calmness, and dependability. It's the serene sky, the vast ocean—both symbols of depth and reliability.

3. Yellow: Optimism, Clarity, Warmth The vibrant color of the sun, yellow often symbolizes positivity, clarity, and warmth. It can energize and revitalize. However, too much yellow or very bright shades can be overwhelming and may induce anxiety.

4. Green: Growth, Health, Harmony Green is the emblematic color of nature, symbolizing growth, freshness, and fertility. It's no wonder that brands emphasizing health, wellness, or environmental consciousness often sport this hue. Moreover, green can also be associated with money and prosperity.

5. Purple: Royalty, Mystery, Luxury In ancient times, purple dye was expensive and often reserved for royalty. Today, purple carries connotations of luxury, sophistication, and mystery. It's also occasionally linked with spirituality.

6. Orange: Enthusiasm, Creativity, Success A blend of the energy of red and the cheerfulness of yellow, orange is a color of enthusiasm, encouragement, and creativity. Brands that wish to exude a sense of youthful energy and innovation often gravitate towards this hue.

7. Black: Elegance, Power, Formality Black is classic and timeless. It's the color of formal attire, luxury cars, and sophistication. In branding, it can provide a feel of exclusivity and elegance. However, it can also signify mourning or darkness if not used thoughtfully.

8. White: Purity, Simplicity, Innocence White is often associated with purity, simplicity, and cleanliness. In design, it's frequently used as a neutral background color but can also denote a minimalist or modern aesthetic.

Navigating the Rainbow of Choices

For budding entrepreneurs and established businesswomen alike, the choice of color in branding isn't one to be made lightly. It's not just about personal preferences or current trends. The colors representing a brand should echo its ethos, aspirations, and the sentiments it hopes to evoke in its audience.

Moreover, cultural considerations are vital. Colors might be perceived differently across various cultures and regions. For instance, while white is often associated with purity and weddings in many Western cultures, it's linked with mourning in some Eastern traditions.

Lastly, remember that consistency is key. Once you've decided on a color palette that aligns with your brand's personality and goals, be consistent in its application across all your branding materials, from your logo to your website to your packaging.

Embrace the power of colors and let them paint your brand's story in the hearts and minds of your audience.

The Art of Storytelling

At the heart of every iconic brand lies a compelling story. From age-old fables whispered around the campfire to the modern tales shared across social media, stories have been the adhesive binding societies, cultures, and businesses. In the ever-evolving world of branding, storytelling is no longer a mere accessory—it's the couture dress that catches the spotlight.

Why Stories Matter

Let's begin with the basics: the human brain is wired for stories. Neurologically speaking, narratives activate parts of our brain that mere facts and figures cannot.

When we're wrapped up in a story, our brain releases dopamine, the "feel good" neurotransmitter. This makes the information more memorable and the experience more enjoyable.

Stories also forge emotional connections. Ever teared up during a heartfelt commercial or felt a surge of adrenaline from a brand's origin tale? That's the power of narrative. By tapping into emotions, stories build empathy, transforming faceless corporations into relatable entities.

Elements of a Riveting Brand Story

1. Authenticity: At its core, your brand's story should be genuine. Authenticity breeds trust, and trust breeds loyalty. It's not about crafting a perfect tale; it's about sharing your brand's true journey, warts and all.
2. Relatability: Your narrative should resonate with your target audience. It's not about you; it's about them. Frame your story in a way that reflects their aspirations, challenges, and dreams.
3. Conflict and Resolution: Every captivating story has a challenge or conflict, followed by a resolution. Whether it's the obstacles you faced when starting your brand or the problem your product aims to solve, highlighting these elements adds depth and drama.
4. Clear Message: While your story can be intricate and layered, the core message should be clear and concise. What's the central theme or lesson you want your audience to take away?

Incorporating Storytelling in Branding

- Content Marketing: Blogs, videos, podcasts—whichever medium you choose, ensure your content tells a part of your brand's story. It's not just about pushing products but sharing experiences.
- Visual Elements: Imagery is a potent tool for storytelling. From your logo to your advertisements, use visuals that align with and amplify your brand's narrative.
- Customer Testimonials: Nothing tells a story better than a satisfied customer. Share their experiences, stories, and journeys as part of your brand narrative.
- Events and Launches: Make each event or product launch a chapter in your brand's evolving story. Celebrate milestones and share setbacks.
- Social Media: Today's digital age offers brands the platform to be ongoing storytellers. Regular updates, behind-the-scenes glimpses, and real-time engagement can all form part of your narrative.

Remember, every interaction a customer has with your brand adds a sentence, a paragraph, or even a chapter to your brand's ongoing narrative. In a marketplace flooded with products and services, it's the stories that set a brand apart, turning casual customers into loyal brand ambassadors.

Ladies, it's time to become not just entrepreneurs but enchanting raconteurs. Let your brand's story be its most potent tool, weaving a tapestry that both enthralls and endears.

Neuro-marketing Insights

The world of marketing has always been about connecting

with the consumer. But what if we told you that there's a way to peek directly into the consumer's brain, deciphering their subconscious reactions to your campaigns? Welcome to the revolutionary realm of neuro-marketing, where science and marketing coalesce, allowing us to understand better how our brain reacts to stimuli in the marketplace.

The Science Behind the Curtain

Neuro-marketing is grounded in neuroscience. By utilizing techniques like Functional Magnetic Resonance Imaging (fMRI) and Electroencephalography (EEG), marketers can observe how different areas of the brain light up in response to specific advertisements, product designs, or branding efforts. In essence, we're tapping into the brain's raw, unfiltered reactions, bypassing the sometimes unreliable nature of traditional consumer feedback.

Why This Matters

1. Emotions Drive Decisions: While we love to think of ourselves as logical beings, many of our purchasing decisions are emotional. Neuro-marketing allows us to see which parts of the brain, especially those linked to emotions, are activated by particular marketing efforts. Knowing what genuinely resonates can be the key to crafting more effective campaigns.
2. Beyond Words: Ever struggled to articulate why you love a certain product? Sometimes, our brain's reactions are subconscious, something we can't easily put into words. Neuro-marketing helps brands comprehend these non-verbal, often subconscious consumer responses.
3. Optimization: By understanding which elements of a

campaign are most engaging or which parts of a website design keep visitors' attention, brands can optimize their strategies for maximum impact.

Key Takeaways from Neuro-marketing Studies

- First Impressions are Rapid: It takes the brain just 200 milliseconds to form a first impression. This emphasizes the importance of grabbing attention quickly in any marketing material.
- The Power of Visuals: Brain scans show that humans process visuals 60,000 times faster than text. Imagery isn't just a complementary element—it's often the main event.
- Loss Aversion is Real: Studies indicate that the pain of losing something is twice as strong as the joy of gaining something of equivalent value. This insight can be leveraged in marketing strategies, especially in promotions or sales.
- Authentic Emotions Resonate: The brain has a fantastic ability to discern genuine emotions, especially in human faces. Authenticity in ads, with real emotions rather than staged ones, often leads to better consumer engagement.

Towards More Ethical Marketing

It's essential to note that with the immense power of neuro-marketing comes a responsibility. Diving deep into the brain's reactions to influence buying decisions walks a fine line. Ethical considerations must always be at the forefront to ensure that marketing remains a tool for informing and inspiring, not manipulating.

In this whirlwind journey of understanding neuro-marketing,

the underlying message for all budding women entrepreneurs is clear: The brain, with its complex web of neurons and synapses, holds secrets to consumer behavior. By harnessing these insights, you're not just shooting in the dark; you're targeting precisely, backed by science, ensuring that your brand's message doesn't just reach the eyes or ears, but resonates in the very neurons of your target audience.

Alright, ladies, we've just taken a whirlwind tour through the fascinating world of marketing psychology, and if you've stuck with me this far, give yourself a well-deserved pat on the back. Or better yet, treat yourself to that fancy latte or some decadent dark chocolate (the brain loves those endorphins!).

We've dived deep into the intricacies of human behavior, the dance of colors in our emotions, and the very neurons that fire up when we see that irresistible ad for shoes we didn't know we needed. Understanding these principles isn't just about selling or brand-building; it's about appreciating the intricate ballet of stimuli and responses that influence our daily decisions.

I hope you've had as much fun unraveling these mysteries as I have presenting them. As marketers, or even as consumers, knowing what makes us tick is empowering. And as powerful women in the business world, we're all about empowerment, aren't we?

So, as we close this chapter, remember this: Behind every successful marketing campaign, there's a savvy businesswoman wielding the mighty sword of psychology, painting the canvas of the marketplace with strokes of understanding, emotion, and a dash of neuroscience. Stay curious, stay empowered, and keep those neurons firing!

CHAPTER 5:
Mastering Social Media

Social media: where the world converges in the vast expanse of the digital realm. It's a bustling market square where ideas are exchanged, brands are built, and empires are birthed. But more than that, it's an opportunity—a chance to showcase your brand and connect directly with the audience that matters.

Let's dive into an analytical overview of the platforms shaping today's business landscape:

1. Instagram: The visual powerhouse. The beauty of Instagram lies in its ability to weave stories through images. Businesses have an incredible opportunity here to display their products, showcase behind-the-scenes glimpses, and even partner with influencers for a broader reach. With features like Stories, IGTV, and Reels, brands can create a mix of ephemeral and lasting content, striking a balance between immediacy and longevity.
2. LinkedIn: This is the corporate gala of the digital world. A space reserved for thought leadership, industry discussions, and networking. It's not just a platform; it's a community of professionals. For businesses, especially those in the B2B

sector, LinkedIn can be a treasure trove of opportunities. Regular articles, engagement with industry topics, and webinar promotions can set you apart as an authority in your field.

3, TikTok: Disruption in action. Many underestimated TikTok, labeling it as a fleeting trend. Yet, with its incredible engagement rates and global reach, it's an arena for the daring. The challenge? Distilling your brand message into bite-sized, engaging content that resonates with a younger demographic. It's not just about trends but innovation and authenticity.

4. Facebook: A cornerstone of digital marketing. Facebook's versatility is unmatched. From pages to groups, from events to marketplace, it offers a multitude of avenues for brands to engage with their audience. Its robust ad platform also allows for granular targeting, ensuring your message reaches the right eyes.

5. X (formerly Twitter): The takeover by Elon Musk in 2023 transformed Twitter into X, but its essence as a hub for real-time communication remains unchanged. With its concise format, X is where news breaks, opinions form, and trends take off. For brands, X offers a unique opportunity to engage in timely conversations, respond to current events, and position themselves at the forefront of what's happening now. Crafting timely and engaging content is crucial, as is the art of listening. It's a place to get insights directly from your consumers and the broader industry.

6. Pinterest: The vision board of the internet. Pinterest is where aspirations transform into reality. Users flock here for inspiration, from home decor ideas to wedding plans. For brands, particularly those in the lifestyle, fashion, or home sectors, Pinterest is an opportunity to inspire and be discovered. It's less about real-time engagement and more about creating evergreen content that continuously drives

traffic back to your site. Imagery is key here, so invest in high-quality visuals that encapsulate your brand's ethos.

7. Snapchat: In a world driven by permanence, Snapchat dared to go ephemeral. It's a platform that captures the 'in the moment' spirit, making it perfect for limited-time offers, sneak peeks, and behind-the-scenes glimpses. Snapchat resonates particularly well with a younger demographic, offering brands an opportunity to tap into a more youthful, spontaneous audience. With features like Geofilters and Lenses, brands can also create unique, interactive content experiences for their followers.

8. YouTube: The digital realm's video giant. What began as a simple platform for sharing personal videos has evolved into a vast universe of content, from DIY tutorials and vlogs to high-quality web series and educational courses. Boasting over two billion logged-in monthly users, YouTube is more than just a platform; it's a culture, a community, and for many, a career.

9. And Others: The social media scene is ever-changing and new platforms consistently emerge while others seem to vanish into thin air. Whatever your preferred social site - understanding the platform's structure and demographics will help you create consistent branding for your business and reach the right audience.

Remember, the key to social media marketing isn't just understanding the platforms—it's understanding your audience on those platforms. A brand's social media strategy should be fluid, adapting to the ever-changing digital landscape while staying rooted in the core brand message. As we venture further, we'll unravel the intricacies of each platform and give you actionable insights to make your mark. So, here's to not just being another face in the digital crowd, but a beacon that shines through.

Developing Content Strategies for Each Platform

Navigating the world of social media marketing can often feel like trying to speak multiple languages simultaneously. Every platform has its own lingo, its unique audience, and a distinct style of content that performs best. However, the good news is that, with a little bit of strategy and some clear steps, you can master the art of speaking 'social.'

Here's a guide to formulating robust content strategies tailored to each major platform:

1. Instagram: The Visual Diary
   - Objective: Showcase brand aesthetics, connect on a personal level, and create visually compelling narratives.
   - Action Steps:
     - Consistency: Maintain a regular posting schedule, whether it's daily, thrice a week, or weekly.
     - Grid Planning: Use tools like Planoly or Later to visualize your grid before posting.
     - Stories & IGTV: Use these for behind-the-scenes content, Q&A sessions, or longer form content.
     - Engage: Respond to comments, create polls, and engage with other accounts in your niche.

2. LinkedIn: The Professional Network
   - Objective: Establish industry authority, network with professionals, and share company milestones.
   - Action Steps:
     - Thought Leadership: Share insightful articles or videos about industry trends.
     - Network: Regularly connect with industry peers, potential clients, or partners.
     - Company Updates: Celebrate company achievements,

hires, and other news.

3. TikTok: The Entertainment Hub
   - Objective: Engage younger audiences, showcase brand personality, and hop on trending challenges.
   - Action Steps:
     - Trend-Watching: Stay updated on trending sounds and challenges.
     - Authenticity: Let loose a little! This platform rewards genuine and fun content.
     - Collaborate: Partner with creators for wider reach.

4. X (formerly Twitter): The Pulse of the Internet
   - Objective: Engage in real-time conversations, share timely updates, and showcase brand wit.
   - Action Steps:
     - Tweet Regularly: Aim for multiple tweets a day if possible.
     - Engage: Jump into trending topics or host regular Q&A sessions.
     - Polls & Quizzes: Engage your audience with interactive content.

5. Pinterest: The Idea Catalog
   - Objective: Drive traffic to your website, showcase brand aesthetics, and tap into the 'planning' audience.
   - Action Steps:
     - Keyword Strategy: Ensure pins and boards are optimized for search.
     - High-Quality Imagery: Pinterest is visual; your images should be top-notch.
     - Engage: Repin relevant content and engage with other creators.

6. YouTube: The Video Library
   - Objective: Offer in-depth content, tutorials, and brand narratives.
   - Action Steps:
     - Consistent Posting: Whether it's weekly or bi-weekly, stick to a schedule.
     - Engage: Reply to comments, collaborate with other YouTubers, and engage in trending challenges or tags.
     - Optimize: Ensure your video titles, descriptions, and tags are SEO-friendly.

7. Facebook: The Community Builder
   - Objective: Foster community, share updates, and create a space for deeper, meaningful engagement with your audience.
   - Action Steps:
     - Groups are Gold: Consider creating a Facebook Group associated with your brand. It can be a space for users to share experiences, ask questions, and engage more intimately with each other and with you.
     - Live Videos: Embrace the power of Facebook Live. This is a great tool for real-time engagement. You can host Q&A sessions, behind-the-scenes looks, or even product launches. Viewers can interact with you directly, asking questions and leaving comments in real-time.
     - Engaging Content: Facebook's algorithm prioritizes posts that generate interaction. This means questions, polls, and content that sparks conversation will be shown to more of your followers organically.
     - Events: If you have any upcoming webinars, sales, or other events, create an event page on Facebook. This keeps your audience notified and allows them to express their interest or even invite others.

- Advertise Strategically: Given its vast user base, advertising on Facebook can offer a significant return on investment. Use targeted ads to reach specific demographics. Regularly review and adjust based on performance metrics.
- High-Quality Imagery and Videos: While it's a given across all platforms, on Facebook, visual content particularly stands out. Share images of your products, behind-the-scenes shots, and other visually appealing content.

As you tailor your content to each platform, always remember the Golden Rule of Content Marketing: Value first, promotion second. Follow the 90/10 rule. 90% value, 10% marketing. Your primary objective should always be to provide value to your audience, whether it's through entertainment, education, or inspiration. When your followers feel seen, heard, and valued, they're more likely to turn into loyal customers and passionate brand advocates. And isn't that the dream?

Universal Content Strategies for Diverse Platforms:

1. Know Your Audience:
   - Action: Conduct audience research for each platform. Understand the demographics, behaviors, and preferences of your followers on each channel.
   - Why It Matters: Different platforms may have slightly different user bases. Content should resonate with the specific audience of that platform.
2. Content Calendars are Key:
   - Action: Develop a content calendar for each platform. This ensures consistent posting and helps in planning content around special dates or events.

- Why It Matters: Consistency is essential in social media to keep your brand top-of-mind for your audience.
3. Repurpose, Don't Just Duplicate:
    - Action: While it's efficient to use content across platforms, ensure you adjust and repurpose it to fit each platform's unique style and audience.
    - Why It Matters: Each platform has its language. What works wonders on LinkedIn might flop on TikTok. Adapt accordingly.
4. Engage, Engage, Engage:
    - Action: It's called social media for a reason. Interact with your audience. Respond to comments, engage with their content, create polls or Q&A sessions.
    - Why It Matters: Social algorithms favor profiles that have high engagement, making your posts more likely to be seen.
5. User-Generated Content (UGC):
    - Action: Encourage your community to create content about your brand. Repost or feature these on your profile.
    - Why It Matters: UGC provides authentic reviews of your brand and deepens community trust.
6. Keep Abreast of Trends:
    - Action: Stay updated with current events and popular culture. Incorporate relevant trends into your content.
    - Why It Matters: It keeps your brand current and relatable, showing your audience that you're in the loop.
7. A/B Testing:
    - Action: Periodically test different content styles, captions, post times, etc., to see what yields the best results.
    - Why It Matters: This constant refinement ensures that your strategies are always optimized.
8. Use Analytics:
    - Action: Regularly check the analytics provided by each platform to gauge the performance of your posts.

- Why It Matters: Analytics provide insights into what's working and what's not, allowing for better strategy refinement.
9. Collaborative Efforts:
    - Action: Partner with brands or influencers that align with your values for joint campaigns or content.
    - Why It Matters: It brings fresh perspectives and reaches new audiences.
10. Continuous Learning and Adaptation:
    - Action: The digital world changes rapidly. Always be in the mindset of learning, adapting, and evolving.
    - Why It Matters: Today's winning strategy might be tomorrow's outdated method. Stay ahead of the curve.

While each platform has its idiosyncrasies, these universal strategies act as the backbone for effective social media marketing. Remember, it's about genuine engagement and delivering value to your audience. Stay true to your brand, understand your followers, and always be prepared to adapt and grow.

Organic Growth: The Natural Rise

Organic growth, at its core, is about growing your brand's presence on social media without paying for advertisements. It's akin to grassroots campaigning, letting your brand grow because people genuinely appreciate and engage with your content.

1. Consistency is Key: Every platform rewards consistency. It signals that your brand is active, relevant, and engaging. Regular posting, without sacrificing quality, keeps your brand on the audience's radar.

2. Value-Driven Content: Before posting, always ask, "What's in it for my audience?" Ensure your content offers value, whether it's educational, entertaining, or inspirational.

3. Engage Authentically: Engagement isn't just about responding to comments on your posts. It's also about proactive engagement: commenting on other posts, sharing relevant content, or starting meaningful discussions.

4. SEO and Keywords: Platforms like Pinterest and YouTube heavily rely on search functionality. Understand the keywords relevant to your brand and incorporate them organically into your posts and video descriptions.

5. Collaborations & Partnerships: Team up with complementary brands or influencers. It's a win-win, giving both brands access to a broader audience.

Paid Advertising: Your Ticket to Accelerated Reach

Ads give you a direct route to place your content in front of a potentially vast and targeted audience. When leveraged correctly, it can yield impressive ROI.

1. Know Your Objective: Before spending a dime, define what you want to achieve: Brand awareness? Sales? Website visits? Different objectives may require different types of ads.

2. Targeting is Everything: The beauty of digital ads lies in targeting. You can specify demographics, interests, behaviors, and more. The more precise your targeting, the higher the chances of conversion.

3. Ad Design Matters: Your ad's visuals and copy must be

compelling enough to grab attention amidst the sea of content. Ensure it aligns with the platform's vibe.

4. Monitor & Adjust: Rarely will your first ad be a home run. Use analytics to understand performance, learn, and refine your approach for the next campaign.

5. A/B Testing: Run two versions of an ad with a slight variation (maybe a different image or headline) to see which one performs better. It's a direct insight into what resonates more with your audience.

6. Allocate Budget Wisely: Start with a modest budget. As you understand what works and yields a positive ROI, you can then confidently scale your ad spend.

Balancing the Scales

While both organic growth and paid advertising have their merits, a balanced approach often yields the best results. Organic growth builds genuine, long-term relationships with an audience. In contrast, ads give that immediate boost, making your brand visible to many.

Remember, the realm of social media is both vast and intimate. While the platforms provide the stage, your content and strategies determine the applause. Whether you're weaving organic narratives or strategically placing ads, ensure every move aligns with your brand's essence and the value you wish to offer.

Fleeting Trends and Lasting Strategies

Ah, the ever-evolving world of digital marketing! It's like a bustling fashion week runway. Some styles are breathtakingly fresh, making headlines today but forgotten tomorrow, while others stand the test of time, becoming the beloved classics. Similarly, in marketing, understanding what's a passing trend and what's a core strategy staple is crucial. Let's dissect this, shall we?

Spotting the Trends: The Flashy Newbies

1. Virality and Short-Lived Buzz: Trends often come with a burst of attention. Remember the Ice Bucket Challenge? It was everywhere and then... it wasn't. Such is the nature of trends.
2. Platform-Specific: Snapchat filters, TikTok dance challenges, or Twitter's fleeting "Fleets" often house trends. They cater to the platform's unique audience and functionality.
3. High Risk, High Reward: Trends can be a gamble. Jump on them early, and you could see massive engagement. But there's also the risk of misjudging a trend or its fit with your brand, leading to potential backlash.
4. Requires Quick Action: If you're looking to capitalize on a trend, speed is your ally. Being a latecomer can make your brand seem out-of-touch or inauthentic.

The Staple Strategies: The Timeless Beauties

1. Storytelling: Whether it's 2005 or 2050, humans resonate with stories. It's in our DNA. Crafting a compelling narrative around your brand is a strategy that never fades.
2. Building Relationships: Engaging authentically with your audience, fostering community, and building trust are cornerstones of successful marketing.
3. Quality Over Quantity: No matter the platform or era, consistently producing high-quality content trumps mass-producing mediocre content.

4. Adaptable Brand Identity: While your core brand values and message remain constant, having the flexibility to evolve with the changing digital landscape is a strategy staple.
5. Data-Driven Decision Making: Trends come and go, but the importance of understanding analytics, measuring performance, and refining strategies based on data remains a permanent fixture.

Straddling the Line: Making Both Work for You

Here's where things get interesting. While it's vital to recognize the distinction between trends and staples, the real magic lies in leveraging both.

1. Integration: Use staples as your foundation and weave trends into this stable framework. For example, use a trending hashtag in a post that tells your brand's story.
2. Stay Updated: Keep an ear to the ground. Attend webinars, follow influential digital marketers, and be an active part of online communities. This will give you timely insights into emerging trends.
3. Test and Learn: Not every trend will be a good fit. But that doesn't mean you shouldn't experiment. Small-scale tests can give insights without risking significant resources.
4. Consistency: While you're riding the wave of a new trend, ensure that your staple strategies are running in the background. They ensure long-term growth and stability.

In the dynamic world of social media marketing, where algorithms change as quickly as user preferences, it's a dance between adapting to the new and holding onto the tried and true. The brands that master this balance don't just survive; they thrive.

Analytics and Metrics: What Numbers Truly Matter

We've all been there. Staring wide-eyed at the overwhelming barrage of numbers, charts, and percentages that our social media platforms generously offer us. It feels like being handed a calculator for a poetry class. What do these figures mean, and more importantly, which ones genuinely matter for your brand's growth? Let's demystify the enigma of analytics and metrics.

Not All Metrics Wear Capes

In a world overflowing with data, the key isn't to chase every metric but to understand and focus on the ones that align with your brand's objectives.

1. Vanity Metrics vs. Actionable Metrics:
   - Vanity Metrics are the "feel-good" numbers. They include metrics like 'Likes' or 'Followers.' Sure, they might give your ego a nice little boost, but do they translate to actual business value? Not necessarily.
   - Actionable Metrics are the real MVPs. These are numbers that can guide decisions and strategies. Think conversion rates, engagement rates, or click-through rates. These metrics offer insights into user behavior and preferences.

Key Metrics to Keep an Eye On

1. Engagement Rate: Engagement encompasses likes, comments, shares, and saves. A high engagement rate indicates that your content resonates with your audience. It's a testament to the quality and relevance of what you're putting out there.

2. Conversion Rate: Arguably the king of all metrics. Whether your goal is to sell a product, gain newsletter subscribers, or encourage event sign-ups, the conversion rate tells you how many people took the desired action after engaging with your content.

3. Click-Through Rate (CTR): For those using paid advertising, CTR indicates the percentage of viewers who clicked on your ad. A low CTR might suggest your ad's content or placement needs revisiting.

4. Bounce Rate: Ever walked into a store, taken a quick look around, and left almost immediately? That's what a website "bounce" is. It's when visitors leave your site after viewing only one page. A high bounce rate could indicate issues with site content, design, or user experience.

5. Customer Lifetime Value (CLV): This metric tells you how much net profit you can expect from the entire future relationship with a customer. It's a great way to gauge the long-term value brought in by your marketing efforts.

6. Return on Investment (ROI): The golden metric. It tells you the profitability of a particular marketing activity. If you're spending more than you're getting back, it's time to re-evaluate.

Understanding the 'Why' Behind the Numbers

It's not enough to just know what the numbers are. The magic lies in understanding why they are the way they are. Dive deep. Was there a sudden spike in website visits? Perhaps one of your posts went viral or a celebrity mentioned your product.

Seeing a drop in engagement? Maybe it's related to algorithm changes, or perhaps your content style needs a refresh.

Metrics aren't just numbers; they're stories. They narrate the tale of your brand's journey in the digital realm, with its highs, lows, twists, and turns. While it's essential to celebrate the soaring engagement rates and impressive conversion numbers, don't be disheartened by the occasional slump. After all, every number, good or bad, offers an invaluable lesson. Embrace them, learn from them, and let them guide your brand to unprecedented heights.

Keeping an Eye Out for the Next Big Thing in Social Media

Social media is like the universe: vast, ever-expanding, and always presenting new stars on the horizon. As entrepreneurs, we're not just content creators; we're trend spotters, always on the hunt for the next game-changing platform. So, how can we anticipate what's next and be at the forefront of the next big social wave? Let's dive in.

The Evolutionary Cycle of Social Media

Social media platforms often emerge to fill a void or offer a new angle on communication that existing platforms haven't touched. Remember when Facebook brought 'real identity' to the forefront, making our online and offline worlds collide? Or when TikTok offered a fresh, fun twist to video content? Each platform had a unique proposition that made it stand out.

Why Keeping an Eye Out Matters

1. First-Mover Advantage: Being among the early adopters can provide an edge. Early content creators often experience

more organic growth, as there's less competition and more visibility.
2. Diverse Audience Reach: Different platforms attract varied demographics. By spreading your brand across multiple platforms, you're not putting all your eggs in one basket and can engage a broader audience spectrum.
3. Adaptability: Brands that can quickly pivot and adapt to new platforms showcase their versatility and stay relevant.

Spotting the Next 'Big Thing'

1. Youth Engagement: Young users are often the early adopters of emerging platforms. If you notice a sudden surge in a platform's popularity among younger demographics, it might be the next big thing.
2. Unique Features: Does the platform offer something distinct that's not available elsewhere? Snapchat introduced ephemeral content, and Clubhouse banked on audio-only rooms. These unique selling points can be a sign of potential growth.
3. Buzz in the Industry: If industry insiders, influencers, or tech publications are buzzing about a new platform, it's worth exploring.

A Few Platforms Gaining Traction

1. X (formerly Twitter): With Elon Musk's takeover, X is rejuvenating its platform, introducing new features and drawing in a diverse audience.
2. Vero: Praised for its no-ads and no-algorithms approach, Vero offers a chronological feed, making it a hit among creators tired of the algorithmic whims of other platforms.
3. Mastodon: A decentralized platform, giving the power back to users, has been gaining attention from those wary of the

monopolistic nature of major platforms.

Staying Ahead Without Spreading Too Thin

While it's crucial to keep an eye out for new platforms, it's equally important not to spread your brand too thin. Quality over quantity always wins. It's better to be genuinely active and engaged on a few platforms than to have a dormant presence on many.

The digital landscape is in perpetual motion. While it's exhilarating to ride the wave of new platforms, always remember the core of your brand's message. Platforms come and go, but authentic brand storytelling remains timeless. By keeping your brand's essence consistent, you can fluidly move through the ever-evolving maze of social media, always ready to seize the next big opportunity.

CHAPTER 6:
Authentic Community Building

In the vast world of commerce, there's one truth that remains unchallenged: people buy from people, not faceless corporations. No matter how cutting-edge your product is or how sophisticated your marketing strategy appears, at the end of the day, consumers crave genuine human connection. Building an authentic community around your brand is not just a marketing strategy; it's a profound commitment to forge genuine connections, cultivate trust, and foster a sense of belonging among your audience.

The Cornerstones of Community

- Transparency and Authenticity: Today's savvy consumers can spot a fake from miles away. It's essential to be genuine in your communications, sharing both your brand's successes and learnings. This transparency fosters trust and credibility.

- Engagement: Being active and responsive is crucial. It's one thing to post content, but another to interact with your followers, answer their questions, and appreciate their feedback.

- Shared Values: Your brand's core values should resonate with your community. It's these shared values that foster a deep connection and build brand loyalty.

- Consistent Communication: Regular updates, newsletters, or check-ins keep your community in the loop. But remember, it's not about quantity but the quality of interactions.

Building Blocks of a Flourishing Community

1. Tailored Content: Content that resonates, educates, and entertains is paramount. This is how you offer value and position yourself as a thought leader in your niche.
2. Exclusive Offers: Reward your community with special deals, early-bird offers, or behind-the-scenes glimpses. It's a way of showing appreciation for their loyalty.
3. Feedback Mechanisms: Constructive feedback is gold. Encourage it, cherish it, and act on it. It not only improves your brand but shows your community that their voice matters.
4. Community Events: Hosting webinars, workshops, or even casual meet-ups can strengthen the bond. Virtual or physical, these events foster a deeper connection between your brand and its tribe.

While building a community is rewarding, it's not without its challenges. Moderating discussions, ensuring a positive environment, handling negative feedback with grace, and staying true to your brand promise are some hurdles you might face. The key is to remain committed, be patient, and understand that community-building is a long-term game.

Building an authentic community is akin to tending to a

garden. It requires patience, care, genuine effort, and, most importantly, love. As the gardener of your brand's community, it's up to you to nurture it, cherish its uniqueness, and ensure it flourishes. In the vast digital landscape, this community will be your beacon, guiding you through challenges and celebrating your successes.

The Importance of Engagement

Dive into any digital marketing conference, webinar, or workshop, and there's one word you'll hear echoing through the halls and across the screens: engagement. But what does engagement truly mean for brands, especially in the age of fleeting attention spans and the bombardment of content? More importantly, why does it matter, particularly for female entrepreneurs looking to leave an indelible mark on their industries?

Unpacking Engagement

At its core, engagement isn't just about likes, shares, or comments. It's about cultivating a two-way relationship with your audience. It's the digital equivalent of a coffee chat where both parties are genuinely interested in the conversation, looking forward to the insights, stories, and emotions exchanged.

Engagement signals a deeper connection. It indicates that your content isn't just passing through a feed, but pausing, making your audience think, feel, react, and interact.

Why Engagement is a Game-Changer

1. Trust Building: Every time you engage with an audience

member, you're taking another step in fostering trust. Responding to comments, thanking followers for their insights, or addressing concerns all show that behind the brand façade, there are real people who care.

2. Algorithmic Advantages: Let's face it, platforms like Instagram, LinkedIn, or X (formerly Twitter) love engagement. The more your content sparks genuine interaction, the more likely these platforms are to showcase your content to a broader audience.

3. Richer Insights: Beyond metrics, engagement provides qualitative insights. Through the candid comments, questions, or discussions around your content, you glean a better understanding of your audience's pain points, aspirations, and needs.

4. Building Brand Advocates: Engaged users aren't just passive consumers; they often turn into brand evangelists. They'll vouch for you, defend you in public forums, and bring in more like-minded followers into your community.

Tips for Boosting Engagement

- Ask Questions: Simple yet effective. Asking questions in your posts can prompt responses, initiating meaningful conversations.
- Share User-Generated Content: Celebrate your community by showcasing their content. This not only boosts their morale but also indicates a brand that's community-centric.
- Host AMAs (Ask Me Anything): An informal, candid format where you address questions, concerns, or just have a fun chat. It's a great way to foster real-time engagement.
- Embrace Stories & Reels: Platforms like Instagram offer features like stories and reels that are interactive by design. Polls, quizzes, and Q&A features can be particularly engaging.

- Value Over Volume: Rather than bombarding your audience with content, focus on sharing value-packed, relevant posts that resonate and invite interaction.

In the vast ocean of digital content, engagement is your anchor. It grounds your brand, ensuring you're not adrift, but actively fostering relationships, creating ripples, and making meaningful connections. For the modern woman entrepreneur, mastering engagement isn't just a strategy; it's an art, an expression of her brand's ethos, passion, and commitment to her community.

Case Studies: Brands with a Loyal Customer Base

Loyalty isn't just earned overnight. It's a culmination of consistent effort, understanding, and nurturing of relationships. Let's explore a few brands, some established and some emerging, that have successfully woven a tapestry of trust and loyalty with their audience.

1. Magnolia by Joanna Gaines

Originating from the hit HGTV show "Fixer Upper," Joanna Gaines, along with her husband Chip, created a brand that goes beyond home renovations. Magnolia encompasses a lifestyle that's about simplicity, authenticity, and family. With a blend of social media, a market, a journal, and books, they've created a space where customers feel connected to the brand's core values.

Key Takeaways:
- Authenticity: Joanna's genuine, down-to-earth approach resonates with her audience.
- Diverse Touchpoints: From physical markets to journals,

the brand ensures multiple avenues of connection.

2. Glossier

A modern beauty brand, Glossier emerged from a beauty blog, "Into The Gloss." Instead of just pushing products, they focus on the narrative of skin-first and makeup-second. They champion the individual, prioritizing real customer reviews and spotlighting diverse beauty on their platforms.

Key Takeaways:
- Community-Centric: Glossier often co-creates products based on community feedback.
- Transparency: The brand is open about its product ingredients and ethos.

3. Rupi Kaur

While not a traditional "brand," poet Rupi Kaur has cultivated a massive, dedicated following. With raw, relatable poetry and minimalist illustrations, she's captured the hearts of many, especially young women navigating life, love, and growth.

Key Takeaways:
- Emotional Connection: Rupi's words resonate deeply, establishing a profound emotional bond with readers.
- Consistent Authenticity: Her style, both in visual and written content, remains unwaveringly authentic.

4. Athleta

An activewear brand, Athleta sets itself apart by being inclusive and women-empowered. Their campaigns feature women of all ages, sizes, and backgrounds. The brand also commits to sustainability and female empowerment initiatives.

Key Takeaways:
- Inclusivity: Athleta ensures every woman sees herself in the brand.
- Values-Driven: Their commitment to positive change, both socially and environmentally, endears them to a conscious audience.

Each of these brands, while diverse in their offerings, share common threads—authenticity, a deep understanding of their audience, and a commitment to values. They don't just sell products or services; they offer experiences, connections, and a sense of belonging. For entrepreneurs charting their path, these brands serve as beacons, illustrating that with genuine intent and consistent effort, you can foster a community that doesn't just buy from you, but believes in you.

Building Trust and Credibility

In the labyrinth of business, trust is your most precious commodity. It's the foundation upon which relationships, loyalty, and brand longevity are built. Credibility isn't just a shiny badge you can pin on your brand; it's an essence you cultivate over time. Let's delve into how you can not only construct but also maintain and enhance this trust.

- Start With Authenticity

In today's digital age, audiences have developed an astute radar for pretense. They seek brands that are genuine, transparent, and human. Authenticity doesn't mean perfection; it means being genuine in your brand's promises and actions. Celebrate your milestones, but also be candid about your challenges. Let your audience in on your journey, the highs and the lows, and they'll feel a deeper connection to your story.

- Deliver Consistently

Consistency is the rhythmic heartbeat of credibility. Whether it's the quality of your product, the tone of your communication, or the experience you offer, ensure it's consistent. This predictability fosters a sense of reliability. Your audience should know that each interaction with your brand will uphold the standards they've come to expect.

- Open Channels of Communication

Establish open and clear channels for communication with your audience. Listen to their concerns, feedback, and experiences. The more you engage in active dialogue, the more you demonstrate your commitment to their satisfaction. This not only bolsters trust but provides invaluable insights to further refine and enhance your brand's offerings.

- Education Over Hard Selling

While sales are essential, leading with an educational approach can be more effective in building trust. By offering valuable information, insights, or tips related to your industry, you position your brand as a knowledgeable leader in the field. This approach not only elevates credibility but subtly showcases the value of your products or services.

- Stand By Your Values

Every brand has a set of core values, principles that guide its actions and decisions. Make those values known to your audience and stand by them unwaveringly. In times of controversy or challenge, staying true to these values speaks volumes about your brand's integrity.

- Collect and Showcase Testimonials

Nothing sings praises louder than the positive experiences of satisfied customers. Encourage your clients to share their stories, testimonials, and feedback. Showcase these on your platforms to offer tangible proof of your brand's credibility.

- Always Own Up and Adapt

Mistakes happen. It's not the missteps but how you address them that defines your brand's credibility. Always own up to errors, apologize sincerely, and most importantly, adapt to ensure they don't recur.

Building trust is an art and a commitment. It's an ongoing process, an ever-evolving dance between your brand and its audience. As you grow and evolve, continue to prioritize this trust, and you'll find that it becomes the wind beneath your wings, propelling you to heights unimaginable.

Delving into Niche Communities for Deeper Engagement

The age of generalized mass marketing is fading. Now, the spotlight is on focused, deeply engaged, and dedicated groups: micro-communities. These smaller, niche clusters offer brands an unparalleled opportunity to build meaningful connections, foster loyalty, and understand their target audience's core. Let's explore the magic behind these micro-communities and how they can elevate your brand.

The Essence of a Micro-community

A micro-community is a specialized group bound together by a shared interest, passion, or objective. Unlike vast, generalized audiences, members of a micro-community are deeply connected, often possessing a higher level of expertise and enthusiasm about their shared focus.

Why Micro-Communities Matter

1. Authentic Engagement: Because of their shared passion, members of a micro-community engage more authentically. Their discussions, feedback, and interactions are often more in-depth, providing a wealth of insights for brands.
2. Loyalty Amplified: Micro-communities thrive on trust and shared values. When a brand aligns with these values, it can cultivate a fiercely loyal customer base within these communities.
3. Precision Marketing: Rather than casting a wide net and hoping for the best, brands can tailor their messages specifically to resonate with a micro-community. This leads to better conversion rates and ROI.

Engaging with Micro-Communities

1. Become a Member, Not a Seller: The quickest way to alienate a micro-community is by entering with a blatant sales agenda. Instead, join as an enthusiastic member. Engage, learn, and contribute value.
2. Offer Exclusive Benefits: Micro-communities appreciate exclusivity. Offer them early-bird specials, sneak peeks, or unique experiences that cater to their specific interests.
3. Collaborate on Content: Empower members to co-create content. Whether it's a blog post, a product review, or even a collaborative product launch, this shared ownership fosters deeper engagement.
4. Host Specialized Events: Organize webinars, Q&A sessions, or workshops tailored to the community's specific interests. This not only showcases your commitment but also

positions your brand as an industry leader.

The Rise of Micro-community Platforms

With the increasing value of micro-communities, platforms that cater to them are seeing a surge. Whether it's invite-only groups, specialized forums, or dedicated social media pages, understanding where your target micro-community hangs out is pivotal.

The Power of Community Leaders

Every micro-community often has a few key influencers or leaders. Building relationships with these individuals can be a gateway to deeper engagement with the entire community. Their endorsement carries weight, and their feedback can offer invaluable insights.

In the vast digital landscape, micro-communities are like cozy campfires. They offer warmth, connection, and a sense of belonging. As brands, when we approach these communities with genuine interest and respect, we're invited to sit, share stories, and form bonds that transcend mere transactions.

Diving Deep into Community-Centric Content Creation

The success of any community, online or offline, hinges on its heartbeats: its members. Thus, the content you create should mirror their passions, interests, concerns, and aspirations. This isn't about just selling a product or service, but about fostering a sense of belonging.

Getting to the Heart of the Matter

To truly understand your community, adopt a multi-dimensional approach:
- Engage in Active Listening: Beyond comments and shares, monitor the sentiments, questions, and discussions that arise.
- Humanize Your Content: Strip away the veneer of corporate talk. Speak as one human to another.
- Cultivate an Inclusive Environment: Ensure all voices are heard, and diverse perspectives are celebrated.

Power Up With Engagement Boosters

Engagement isn't just about numbers, but the quality of interaction:
- Interactive Content: Use quizzes, polls, and challenges to foster participation. Transform passive followers into active participants.
- Celebration and Appreciation: Acknowledge community achievements, birthdays, and milestones, making everyone feel seen and valued.
- Guest Takeovers: Invite community members or industry experts for takeovers. This provides fresh perspectives and can be a learning experience for all.

Building Value, Brick by Brick

To remain relevant and authoritative, your content must consistently offer value:
- Continual Learning: Host webinars, workshops, or create eBooks that offer tangible value and knowledge to the community.
- Shine a Spotlight: Feature community members, share their

stories, successes, or testimonies.
- Stay Authentic: Every piece of content should resonate with your brand's core values. Avoid jumping onto every trending topic; instead, focus on what aligns with your community's ethos.

Feedback as a Growth Catalyst

A feedback-driven approach ensures the community stays dynamic and responsive:
- Feedback Channels: Establish clear channels for feedback. Could be monthly roundtables, feedback forms, or suggestion boxes.
- Evolve with Feedback: Don't just collect feedback, act on it. Show your community that their voice matters and shapes the collective journey.

Community-centric content is not a one-off initiative; it's an ongoing commitment. It's about weaving a tapestry of trust, value, and engagement where every thread—every member—holds significance. This commitment, in turn, yields loyalty, word-of-mouth recommendations, and a thriving brand ecosystem.

Feedback Loop: The Pulse of Your Community's Heartbeat

Every thriving community thrives on open channels of communication, and this isn't just a one-way street. The essence of a vibrant community is its continuous ebb and flow of feedback. This invaluable information not only tells you what you're doing right but also sheds light on areas of improvement.

Why Feedback Matters

Imagine navigating a ship without a compass; you're bound to drift aimlessly. Feedback serves as this compass, guiding your brand towards the right path:
- Course Correction: Regular feedback helps in timely course correction before minor issues snowball into bigger problems.
- Building Trust: Demonstrating that you genuinely value and act on feedback strengthens trust among community members.
- Innovation Drive: Fresh perspectives can spark new ideas or solutions you might not have considered.

Methods to Gather Constructive Feedback

Harnessing feedback requires a multi-faceted approach:
- Surveys: A structured set of questions can garner a wealth of insights. Use tools like SurveyMonkey or Google Forms to collate responses.
- Virtual Roundtables: Periodic group discussions offer members a platform to share their thoughts freely.
- Direct Channels: Provide members with direct channels—like email or DMs—ensuring they can reach out whenever they have feedback.
- Feedback Contests: Incentivize feedback by offering rewards or recognitions for the best suggestions or insights.

Feedback Analysis: Moving Beyond Surface Level

Gathering feedback is just the first step. Dive deep to understand the core issues or suggestions:

- Identify Patterns: Look for recurring themes or common points in the feedback. This indicates areas that need immediate attention.
- Categorize Feedback: Break feedback into categories—like product improvement, content suggestions, community events—to streamline the action process.
- Prioritize: Some feedback might require immediate attention, while others could be part of long-term strategies.

Acting on Feedback: Show, Don't Just Tell

Simply collecting feedback won't suffice; the community needs to see tangible action:
- Regular Updates: Keep the community in the loop about the changes you're implementing based on their feedback.
- Success Stories: Share instances where feedback led to significant improvements or innovations. This not only reinforces the value of feedback but also motivates more members to participate actively.
- Acknowledge and Appreciate: Recognize individuals whose feedback led to notable changes. This could be through shout-outs, badges, or even tangible rewards.

The feedback loop isn't a mere process; it's a commitment. It says, "We're listening, we value your input, and we're ready to grow with you." By actively seeking, valuing, and applying feedback, you're not just building a product or a brand—you're nurturing a thriving, engaged, and loyal community.

Well, there we have it—a deep dive into the captivating world of community building. As we've journeyed together through these pages, it's evident that community isn't just about numbers or hollow interactions. It's the heartfelt engagements, the trust we cultivate, the feedback we cherish, and the authentic connections we foster.

Remember, every thriving business empire—no matter how vast—started as a small, close-knit community. It's the magic of this genuine bond that propels a brand to incredible heights. As you move forward, think of your community not just as a business asset, but as a living, breathing entity that grows, evolves, and enriches your brand's journey.

Keep those engagement vibes high, value every piece of feedback, and never underestimate the power of a well-connected community. Here's to building not just a brand, but a family that stands by it.

CHAPTER 7:
Effective Networking

Picture this: You're at a lavish business gala, decked out in your most empowering outfit. The chandelier above glistens, casting a warm glow over the room. You clutch your glass of sparkling water with a twist of lime, ready to mingle and make connections. Why? Because you know the power of networking. You're not just there for the appetizers (though they're a delicious bonus); you're there to build bridges.

The True Essence of Networking

Let's dispel a common myth right off the bat—networking isn't just about handing out business cards willy-nilly or flaunting your achievements. It's about genuine connections. It's the art of recognizing mutual potential and building relationships that bring value to both parties. Think of it as a tango: it's a dance of give and take.

Networking is a two-way street. The magic happens when it's not all about "What can you do for me?" but "How can we collaborate and elevate each other?" That's the kind of synergy that paves the way for genuine partnerships and collaborations.

Why Women Rock at Networking

Let's face it, ladies—we're naturally excellent communicators. We're empathetic, intuitive, and have an innate ability to read between the lines. These qualities aren't just fantastic for friendships and family; they're powerful assets in the business realm.

Studies have consistently shown that women are adept at building long-term, meaningful relationships. When we network, it's not just transactional—it's transformational. We delve deeper, seeking not just professional connections but shared visions and values.

Seeking and Nurturing Partnerships

Beyond individual networking, the journey of scaling and expanding often requires the support of partnerships. Think of partnerships as business besties—you're in it together, through thick and thin.

But how do you find the right fit? Start by identifying brands or individuals whose values align with yours. It's like finding a puzzle piece that fits just right. Next, nurture the relationship. Open up a dialogue, share ideas, and see if there's chemistry. A thriving partnership isn't just about shared goals, but shared values and trust.

From Networking to Net-Worth

Here's a nugget of wisdom: Your net-worth often mirrors your network. The connections you make today can open doors tomorrow. So, be genuine, be open, and be ready to embark on exciting collaborations that can propel both parties to new heights.

Remember, every interaction is an opportunity to learn, to grow, and to expand your horizons. So, put on those fabulous heels, step into the room with confidence, and remember: You're not just networking, you're net-worth-ing!

In the pages that follow, we'll delve into the nitty-gritty of leveraging connections, exploring collaborative marketing, and forming partnerships that stand the test of time.

Leveraging Connections to Expand Reach

You're standing at the edge of a serene, placid pond. With a gentle flick of your wrist, you toss a stone into the water. The initial splash might be small, but the ripples it creates extend far and wide. Each ripple represents an opportunity, a connection, and a potential collaboration. In the world of business, you are that stone, and your network represents that pond. Each connection you nurture has the potential to create ripples that expand your reach beyond your wildest dreams.

It's Not Just Who You Know, But How You Know Them

We've all heard the adage, "It's not what you know, but who you know." But here's the twist: It's not just about having a Rolodex bursting with contacts; it's about the depth and quality of those relationships. A genuine connection with a handful of key individuals can be more potent than superficial ties with hundreds.

When you establish trust and build rapport, these individuals become your advocates. They're not just contacts—they're allies, ready to vouch for you, introduce you to their network,

network, and potentially catapult you into opportunities you hadn't even considered.

Strategic Networking: A Game of Chess, Not Checkers

Effective networking is strategic. It's not about attending every event or joining every club. Instead, it's about discerning where your energy will be most productive and then diving deep.

Ask yourself: Who are the pivotal players in my industry? Where are the spaces and events they frequent? Which platforms do they engage with most? Then, position yourself strategically in those arenas.

But here's the golden rule: Always lead with value. How can you support them? Can you offer insights, share resources, or make introductions that could benefit them? When you approach connections with a genuine desire to provide value, you not only build trust but also create a foundation for mutual growth.

The Ripple Effect: Beyond the Immediate Connection

Every individual you connect with possesses their unique network, insights, and experiences. When you establish a relationship with one person, you indirectly tap into their entire world of connections. It's a beautiful, cascading effect where one introduction can lead to a plethora of opportunities.

The next time you're at a networking event, conference, or even a casual coffee catch-up, remember the power you hold. You're not just building a bridge to one person; you're opening doors to an entire universe of opportunities.

Collaborative Marketing and Brand Partnerships

In the ever-evolving business landscape, collaborative marketing and brand partnerships have emerged as powerful tools for companies to amplify their reach and redefine their narratives. It's more than a mere fusion of logos or sharing a mutual audience; it's about forging meaningful connections.

Defining the Power Duo

- Collaborative Marketing: This is the heart of synergy. Two brands merging their strengths to craft campaigns or initiatives that hold a unique, compelling proposition for their audience. It's not just about sharing a platform but adding value to each other's brand story.
- Brand Partnerships: This is where innovation meets brand essence. A fusion of two identities, it can be a limited edition product, an event, or a long-term partnership. The idea is to create a new experience that captivates and retains the collective audience of both brands.

Blueprint for a Successful Collaboration

Venturing into a collaborative space can be a strategic move for brands, but it's crucial to navigate this journey wisely. Here's a guideline:

- Value Alignment: Ensure that both brands have compatible values and missions. This forms the foundation of any successful partnership.
- Clear Communication: Transparency is vital. Be upfront about expectations, potential challenges, and the shared vision.

- Joint Objectives: Define clear goals. Whether it's tapping into a new demographic or amplifying brand awareness, having shared targets helps streamline efforts.
- Mutual Respect and Admiration: Understand and appreciate the strengths of your partner brand. This mutual respect is the glue that binds successful collaborations.
- Evaluation and Growth: Once the campaign wraps up, take the time to analyze the outcomes. Understand the hits and misses, and use this knowledge for future collaborations.

In a world teeming with brands vying for the spotlight, collaborations offer an avenue to break through the noise. They allow brands to offer fresh perspectives, products, and experiences to their audience.

And as you ponder the myriad possibilities of partnerships, remember: it's not about losing your brand's identity but enriching it. A successful collaboration results in a win-win situation for both brands, giving consumers something novel and exciting. So, embrace the collaborative spirit, and you might just discover your brand's next groundbreaking venture.

The Power of a Strong Introduction

It's a familiar scenario for most entrepreneurs: you stumble across someone you believe would be a perfect fit for a collaboration, mentorship, or even a potential client. But there's a small hurdle - they have no idea who you are.

That's where cold outreach comes in. The key? Making that first impression count.

The Three C's of Cold Outreach

1. Clarity:
   - Purpose Driven: Know what you want. Whether it's a mentorship opportunity, collaboration, or a business deal, be transparent about your intentions.
   - Short and Sweet: Time is gold. Deliver your message succinctly, ensuring that the key points stand out.
2. Confidence:
   - Know Your Worth: Understand and believe in the value you bring. Your confidence will resonate.
   - Rejections? No Sweat!: Not every outreach will turn into a connection. Embrace rejection and view it as a learning opportunity.
3. Consistency:
   - Follow Up: Sometimes emails get lost, or the recipient is too busy. A gentle reminder can nudge them towards a response.
   - Iterate: Continuously refine your approach based on feedback and results. What works today might need a tweak tomorrow.

Tactics to Elevate Your Outreach Game

- Human Touch: Start with a personal note. Maybe you loved their recent article or product launch. Make it genuine.
- Stand Out: Use catchy subject lines or openers that pique curiosity without being overly flashy.
- Value Proposition: Clearly state what you bring to the table. What's in it for them?
- Visual Aid: Consider adding infographics, portfolio links, or relevant attachments to enhance your pitch.
- Call to Action: End with a clear CTA. Maybe you'd like a quick chat, a meeting, or their feedback on something.

And here's the golden rule: treat cold outreach as a conversation starter, not a sales pitch. It's an introduction, a handshake if you will. You're not trying to seal the deal immediately but aiming to start a dialogue. So, approach it with openness, humility, and a genuine desire to connect. After all, the most fruitful business relationships often begin with a simple 'hello.'

Planting the Seed: The Initial Connection

Building a network is akin to tending a garden. The initial connection is merely the act of planting a seed. But without continuous care and nourishment, that seed will fail to grow, or worse, wither away. The art of nurturing relationships in your network is a deliberate and thoughtful process, one that requires genuine effort and time.

Cultivating Your Connection: A Consistent Approach

1. Regular Check-ins: Like watering a plant, it's essential to touch base with your contacts periodically. It can be a simple email, a phone call, or even a lunch meet-up. The idea is to keep the connection alive.
2. Celebrate Milestones: Whether it's a job promotion, a business win, or even personal accomplishments like anniversaries or birthdays. A short congratulatory message can go a long way.
3. Lend a Hand: Opportunities to assist might arise, whether they're looking for recommendations, advice, or resources. Be proactive in your willingness to help.
4. Engage Authentically: Avoid the trap of only reaching out when you need something. Authentic engagement means showing interest without any underlying motives.

The Importance of Reciprocity

At its core, a fruitful professional relationship should be mutual. The give-and-take dynamics ensure both parties benefit, fostering trust and respect. If you find that the balance is tipped more on one side—whether it's yours or theirs—it's time for a check-in to realign.

Shared Experiences: Beyond Work

Engage in activities outside the professional realm. Attend workshops, seminars, or even social events together. Shared experiences can strengthen bonds and offer fresh perspectives on each other.

Navigating Challenges

Every relationship faces its set of challenges. Perhaps there's a disagreement or a lull in communication. The key is to address issues head-on. Open dialogue, understanding, and compromise are the cornerstones of maneuvering through such hiccups.

To sum up, maintaining long-term relationships within your network isn't a one-time task—it's an ongoing commitment. Like a gardener tending to their plants, you must nurture, care for, and occasionally prune your connections to ensure a thriving network that will support you throughout your entrepreneurial journey.

The Untapped Goldmine of Networking

In the age of digital connections, the power of face-to-face interactions at events, conferences, and summits cannot be understated. These gatherings are hotspots for building relationships, exchanging knowledge, and even initiating collaborations. But, like any goldmine, it's all about knowing where to dig and how to extract the value.

Strategies Before the Event

1. Set Clear Objectives: Determine what you aim to achieve. Whether it's connecting with potential clients, seeking partners, or simply gaining industry insights, having a goal will give your presence direction.
2. Research the Attendees and Speakers: Familiarize yourself with notable attendees and key speakers. This knowledge can serve as conversation starters and will help you identify whom you'd like to meet.
3. Prepare an Elevator Pitch: Have a concise and compelling introduction ready. This should encapsulate who you are, what you do, and what value you bring.
4. Business Card 101: Always carry enough business cards. Ensure they are current and reflect your brand accurately.

Making the Most of the Event

- Engage Actively in Sessions: Participate by asking questions and sharing insights. Being vocal (without overdoing it) positions you as an engaged and informed attendee.
- Network Intentionally, Not Broadly: Instead of trying to meet everyone, focus on fostering deep connections with a select few. Quality over quantity.
- Utilize Breaks Efficiently: Coffee breaks, lunchtimes, and cocktail hours are prime networking opportunities. Use this time to approach speakers or initiate conversations with fellow attendees.

- Take Notes: Jot down key takeaways from sessions and important details about the people you meet. This will aid in post-event follow-ups.

Post-Event Actions

1. Follow-up Promptly: Send out personalized emails or messages to the contacts you made, preferably within 48 hours. Mention specific conversations you had to jog their memory.
2. Connect on Social Media: Add your new contacts on platforms like LinkedIn or X. This keeps the connection alive and facilitates future interactions.
3. Evaluate Your Performance: Reflect on what went well and what didn't. Did you meet your objectives? Use these insights to improve for future events.

Continuous Engagement

Don't let the relationship end with the event. Engage with your new contacts by sharing relevant articles, congratulating them on achievements, or even proposing a catch-up call or meet-up.

Stepping into the world of business as a woman can sometimes feel like venturing into uncharted waters. But remember this: it's not just about what you know, but who you know. As we've journeyed through this chapter, one thing becomes incredibly clear – the power of human connections can never be undervalued.

From leveraging existing ties to embarking on cold outreaches, and from the intimate beauty of micro-collaborations to the vast opportunities in events – every interaction presents a chance. A chance to learn, to grow, to collaborate, and to elevate.

Networking isn't merely transactional. It's relational. It's about fostering genuine connections, understanding mutual goals, and growing together. So, as you turn the page, hold close the insights from this chapter and approach networking with an open heart, a keen mind, and a spirit ready to connect.

Here's to bridges yet to be built and partnerships waiting to shape the future!

CHAPTER 8:

Financial Intelligence

Money. It's the lifeblood of every business and, whether we like it or not, plays a pivotal role in determining the success and longevity of our entrepreneurial endeavors. The world of finance, with its numbers and charts, can seem daunting. Especially in a society that, historically, hasn't always empowered women to take charge of their financial destinies. But, times are changing, and you, dear reader, are at the forefront of this shift.

Welcome to a chapter that promises to be both enlightening and empowering. Here, we demystify the complexities of financial management, break down the essentials, and provide you with the tools to not only understand but to thrive in the financial aspect of your business.

Because let's face it, passion and dedication are the soul of your venture, but financial intelligence? That's the backbone. It's the tool that transforms dreams into realities, and ambitions into sustainable, long-term successes.

From understanding cash flow to mastering the art of ROI, we'll journey together through the financial maze, ensuring that by the end of this chapter, you'll wear your financial knowledge not just as a skill, but as an armor. Let's dive into the world of numbers, charts, and balances with confidence and grace, and ensure that your business stands on a foundation as solid as your ambition.

Decoding the Financial Triad: Cash Flow, Profit Margins, and ROI

In the realm of business finance, there's a trinity of terms that reign supreme: Cash Flow, Profit Margins, and ROI (Return on Investment). Each of these terms is crucial to the financial health of your venture. Think of them as the vital signs doctors check during a medical examination. So, let's put on our financial physician hats and delve deep into this triad.

1. Cash Flow – The Business's Pulse Every thriving business has one thing in common: a healthy, steady pulse of money flowing in and out. This is what we call cash flow. It's the movement of money into your business (inflows) and out of it (outflows). Keeping a close eye on this ensures that you always have enough cash on hand to cover your immediate expenses.

- Positive Cash Flow: When more money flows into the business than out of it.
- Negative Cash Flow: When the outflows of cash are greater than the inflows. While occasional negative cash flows aren't a death knell, consistent ones are a red flag.

Tip: Regularly updating and reviewing a cash flow statement helps you spot patterns, anticipate future cash needs, and avoid potential shortfalls.

2. Profit Margins – The Measure of Efficiency While cash flow gauges your business's financial health, profit margins measure its efficiency. In simple terms, it's the percentage of total sales revenue that translates into profit.

Here's a quick formula:
Profit Margin = (Net Profit / Sales) x 100

For instance, if you sold products worth $1000 and made a net profit of $200, your profit margin would be 20%.

Remember, a higher profit margin indicates a more profitable company that has better control over its costs compared to its competitors. Keeping tabs on industry-average profit margins gives you a benchmark to aim for or surpass.

3. ROI – The Accountability Check Every investment you make in your business, be it time, money, or resources, should bring a return. That's where ROI comes into play. It's a metric that evaluates the profitability of an investment.

Here's how you calculate it:
ROI = (Net Profit from the Investment - Cost of the Investment) / Cost of the Investment

Suppose you spent $500 on a marketing campaign that led to $1500 in sales. The net profit, after subtracting the cost, is $1000. Thus, the ROI would be 2, or 200%. This means you earned twice what you invested.

Golden Nugget: Regularly analyzing your ROI helps in assessing which investments are paying off and which aren't. If a strategy isn't delivering, it might be time to pivot.

By now, you should have a clearer picture of these vital financial metrics. Remember, keeping a keen eye on these three will ensure that your business not only survives but thrives and grows. They're not just numbers; they're the narrative of your business's financial journey.

Mapping Your Financial Future: The Essence of Planning and Expert Guidance

Let's start with a truth we all know: Every journey, especially a business one, benefits from a well-defined map. In the world of business, this map is your financial plan, a roadmap detailing how funds will be spent and earned. But here's the catch: Even with the best map in hand, if you don't understand the terrain or the possible hurdles ahead, you may find yourself veering off course. That's where the wisdom of a seasoned guide, a financial expert, becomes invaluable.

Crafting Your Financial Blueprint

Financial planning isn't just about numbers and spreadsheets; it's about setting clear objectives and charting the best course to achieve them. A robust financial plan can:

- Illuminate Goals and Milestones: By identifying and setting clear financial objectives, you're not shooting in the dark. You have a target, whether it's a revenue goal, an expansion plan, or a desired profit margin.
- Optimize Resource Allocation: It ensures that every dollar is used efficiently, maximizing its impact, whether it's allocated for operations, marketing, hiring, or R&D.
- Forecast Potential Challenges: Financial planning allows you to anticipate potential cash flow issues, market downturns, or unexpected expenses, preparing you to

handle them efficiently.
- Guide Decision-Making: With a clear financial picture, every business decision, be it big or small, can be made with an understanding of its potential impact.

The Value of an Expert's Eye

While entrepreneurial spirit and grit are commendable, there's no substitute for expert advice when navigating complex financial landscapes. Here's why seeking it out can be transformative:

1. Depth of Experience: Financial advisors have seen the patterns, pitfalls, and successes. Their insights can help steer you clear of common mistakes and towards proven strategies.
2. Objective Analysis: An external expert can provide a fresh, unbiased perspective on your finances, free from emotional attachment.
3. Specialized Knowledge: The financial world is vast. From tax intricacies to investment opportunities, a specialist can guide you in areas outside your expertise.
4. Peace of Mind: Knowing that a professional is looking after your finances, or at least guiding your hand, can alleviate some of the immense stress that comes with running a business.

In Action: Imagine wanting to explore a foreign land. Would you feel more confident with just a map or with a map and a guide who's traveled that terrain countless times? The latter, right? That's precisely the relationship between financial planning and expert advice.

To thrive in the intricate dance of entrepreneurship, especially as a woman breaking barriers and reshaping industries, it's essential to balance confidence in your intuition with the humility to seek counsel. Harness both, and watch your financial landscape transform from a maze of numbers into a strategic gameboard, where you're always several moves ahead.

Investment Strategies for Startups: Navigating the Waters of Wise Spending

Stepping into the world of entrepreneurship, one quickly realizes that money isn't just a resource—it's a tool. How you wield this tool, especially in the startup phase, can greatly influence your business trajectory. While the entrepreneurial journey is filled with countless decisions, discerning where and when to invest stands out as crucial.

The Golden Rule: Return on Investment (ROI)

Before diving into the specifics, always hold the principle of ROI close. Every dollar you put into your business should be viewed as an investment with an anticipated return. This mindset will guide you to make more calculated decisions, rather than merely spending.

1. Product or Service Development

Your product or service is the backbone of your startup. Early-stage investment in research, development, and refinement can set the foundation for everything that follows. This includes prototyping, beta testing, and market research to ensure your offering meets consumer needs and stands out in the marketplace.

Action Step: Allocate resources to improve your product based on feedback. It could be a design tweak, additional features, or even an entirely new iteration.

2. Marketing and Branding

Without visibility, even the best products can languish. Investing in marketing, especially digital strategies, can amplify your reach. Simultaneously, branding efforts will help define your business's identity, fostering trust and recognition.

Action Step: Consider partnering with marketing professionals or agencies that specialize in startups or your specific industry.

3. Talent Acquisition

The right team can make or break your startup. Investing in skilled individuals who share your vision not only strengthens your operations but also fosters a collaborative environment.

Action Step: Prioritize roles that are pivotal in the initial stages. For instance, if you're launching a tech platform, onboard a solid tech team before focusing on other areas.

4. Technology and Infrastructure

In today's digital age, a robust online presence and smooth operational tech are non-negotiable. From a user-friendly website to efficient CRM tools, ensure your tech infrastructure aligns with your business goals.

Action Step: Explore SaaS (Software as a Service) tools tailored for startups. They often come with flexible pricing and scalability.

5. Continuous Learning and Training

The business landscape is ever-evolving. Investing in ongoing education for yourself and your team ensures you stay ahead of industry shifts and trends.

Action Step: Dedicate a budget for workshops, online courses, and conferences. Encourage knowledge-sharing sessions within the team.

6. Financial Cushion

Startups often face unforeseen expenses. Having a financial buffer can help navigate these without jeopardizing operations.

Action Step: Aim to maintain a reserve fund, enough to cover 3-6 months of operational costs.

Timing is Everything

While knowing where to invest is essential, understanding the timing can optimize your outcomes. For instance, pouring money into aggressive marketing before refining your product might not yield the best results.

Think of your startup as a growing plant. While water, sunlight, and nutrients are all essential, each has its time and place. Overwatering or excessive sunlight can harm rather than help. Similarly, strategic investment—knowing what your startup needs and when—can be the difference between thriving and merely surviving.

Expanding Your Wealth: Using Investment For Passive Income For Growth

The allure of the entrepreneur's journey isn't just about establishing a successful business. It's also about creating sustainable wealth for the long haul. One potent way to do this? Passive income. Picture this: a river that, once set in motion, continues to flow, bringing you steady income without the constant, hands-on effort of your primary venture. Real estate is a prime candidate for this type of revenue stream, and here's why.

Real Estate: The Evergreen Investment

Throughout history, land and property have been seen as some of the most resilient and rewarding investments. They offer both stability and appreciating value over time.

1. Rental Properties

The Basics: This involves purchasing a property and renting it out. It could be residential, like apartments or houses, or commercial spaces such as office buildings or retail shops.

Why It Works: With a well-maintained property in a growing area, you not only receive monthly rent (your passive income) but over time, the property itself can increase in value.

Action Step: Start by researching emerging neighborhoods or towns with growth potential. Look for areas with planned infrastructure upgrades, new schools, or burgeoning commercial centers.

2. Real Estate Investment Trusts (REITs)

The Basics: REITs are companies that own, operate, or finance income-generating real estate across a range of sectors. By investing in a REIT, you're essentially buying shares of a company that manages a collection of properties.

Why It Works: REITs are accessible. Unlike buying property, which requires a significant amount of capital, REITs allow investors to start with a smaller amount. Plus, they pay dividends!

Action Step: Diversify by investing in multiple REITs that focus on different sectors: residential, commercial, industrial, or even specialized areas like healthcare facilities.

3. Property Flipping

The Basics: This strategy involves buying a property, renovating it, and selling it at a profit.

Why It Works: With a keen eye for potential, a property can be transformed and sold for significantly more than its purchase price. However, this approach requires more hands-on effort than the others.

Action Step: If you're new to flipping, consider partnering with a seasoned pro for your first few ventures. Learn the ropes and minimize rookie mistakes.

Beyond Real Estate: While real estate stands tall as a reliable passive income stream, diversifying your investments is wise. Consider exploring other avenues like dividend-paying stocks, peer-to-peer lending or even creating digital products or courses related to your business expertise.

Think of passive income as a symphony. While your business might be the lead violin, passive income sources, like real estate, can fill the hall with rich, harmonious sound, elevating your wealth-building orchestra. By strategically selecting and investing, you're not just building wealth; you're crafting a legacy.

Avoiding Common Financial Pitfalls: Lessons Learned from Past Mistakes

When venturing into the realm of entrepreneurship, it's not just about the successes we should be looking at. As much as we admire the glossy magazine cover stories, the tales of hardships, stumbles, and outright blunders are where the real gold lies. These stories aren't just about the mistakes but also about the comebacks, the resilience, and the lessons learned.

1. Overextending Yourself Financially

It's tempting, especially in the early stages, to pump every dollar back into the business. New equipment, marketing campaigns, hiring – the list seems endless. But stretching yourself too thin can lead to tremendous stress and potential financial ruin.

Lesson Learned: Always keep a reserve. A financial cushion can be your saving grace during lean months or unexpected downturns.

Action Step: Create a separate business savings account and commit to setting aside a percentage of your monthly income. Think of it as insurance for your entrepreneurial journey.

2. Not Keeping Tabs on Expenses

From that unplanned software subscription to the occasional business lunch, expenses can quickly add up. Without keeping track, you can find yourself burning through cash at an alarming rate.

Lesson Learned: Every penny counts. Being lackadaisical with tracking expenses can create significant financial blind spots.

Action Step: Invest in reliable accounting software. Schedule regular financial check-ins, be it weekly or monthly, to ensure you're on top of your expenditure.

3. Avoiding Professional Financial Help

We get it. In the beginning, it's all about bootstrapping. But as your business grows, financial complexity can grow with it.

Lesson Learned: There's value in seeking out expertise. A professional can offer insights and strategies you might not have considered.

Action Step: Engage a financial advisor or accountant familiar with your industry. Even if it's just a quarterly check-in, their guidance can be invaluable.

4. Putting All Eggs in One Basket

Whether it's relying too heavily on a single client or not diversifying your investments, this approach can leave you vulnerable.

Lesson Learned: Diversity equals stability. By spreading your risk, you're better positioned to weather unexpected storms.

Action Step: Regularly assess your client portfolio and investment strategies. Look for opportunities to branch out and expand.

5. Ignoring Financial Education

Entrepreneurship is a journey of constant learning. While you might be an expert in your field, financial literacy is equally crucial.

Lesson Learned: Knowledge is power, especially when it comes to finances. The more you know, the better decisions you'll make.

Action Step: Dedicate time for financial education. Attend workshops, read books, or take online courses.

It's crucial to remember that everyone makes mistakes. The power lies not in avoiding them altogether but in how we respond, adapt, and grow from these experiences. As you navigate the financial seas of entrepreneurship, take these lessons to heart. They might just save you a lot of time, money, and heartache.

Taxation and Legal Insights: Navigating the Intricate World of Business Laws

"Taxation without representation!" That was a rallying cry from centuries ago, but today's entrepreneur might feel it should be, "Taxation without comprehension!" Taxes, laws, regulations — all the bureaucratic details can feel like navigating a labyrinth. But with a bit of guidance and clear understanding, we can demystify this realm.

The Basics: Know Your Tax Types

Understanding taxes starts with knowing what you're being taxed on. Here are a few key categories:

- Income Tax: Based on the business's profit. Varies depending on your business structure, from sole proprietorships to corporations.
- Sales Tax: If you're selling goods, especially at a retail level, be prepared to collect sales tax. Rates can vary significantly across states and even cities.
- Payroll Tax: Employing others? You'll be responsible for withholding, and often matching, certain taxes from their pay.

Legal Structures and Their Impacts

Your business's legal structure, whether it's a sole proprietorship, LLC, or corporation, can significantly influence your tax implications.

- Sole Proprietorships and Partnerships: Typically, profits and losses flow through to the individual's tax return.
- Corporations: These entities pay their own taxes. Owners or shareholders then pay taxes on dividends or salaries they receive.
- LLCs: A bit of a hybrid, allowing owners flexibility in how they're taxed. They can opt for taxation like a sole proprietorship, partnership, or corporation.

Deductions: Your Financial Friends

Here's where things get fun. Well, as fun as taxes can be. Deductions reduce the amount of income that's considered taxable. Common ones include:

- Home Office Deduction: Got a dedicated workspace in your home? There's a deduction for that.
- Travel and Meals: Business trips and certain meals can be written off.
- Education and Training: Classes and workshops to enhance your business skills? Deductible.

Seeking Guidance: The Power of Professionals

Taxes and legal regulations are complex. Even with all your entrepreneurial gusto, there's no shame in seeking help.

- CPAs and Accountants: These folks are wizards with numbers and can ensure you're optimizing your financial situation while staying compliant.
- Attorneys: Especially if you're in a specialized or highly regulated industry, having a legal expert in your corner is invaluable.

In this dance of numbers and regulations, staying informed is your first line of defense against potential pitfalls. Still, the real power move? Leveraging professionals who can guide you through the nuances, ensuring you not only stay on the right side of the law but also utilize it to bolster your business's financial health. After all, as the saying goes: "It's not about how much you make, but how much you keep."

Diving into the depths of financial intelligence and management can often feel like navigating uncharted waters. But armed with the insights from this chapter, you're no longer a novice sailor but a capable captain of your ship.

Understanding cash flows, ROI, investment strategies, and the intricacies of taxes and laws isn't just about avoiding pitfalls. It's about steering your business vessel toward more prosperous horizons, leveraging the winds of knowledge to propel you forward. As women in business, we don't shy away from challenges; we equip ourselves to meet them head-on.

Always remember: Financial acumen isn't about innate ability but learned expertise. Keep educating yourself, seeking advice when needed, and always staying proactive in your approach. Your business's financial health is a testament to your dedication and resilience. Go on and make those numbers work for you, just as you've been doing in every other aspect of your journey.

CHAPTER 9:

Scaling and Expansion

The entrepreneurial journey is akin to climbing a mountain. Initially, the path is steep, fraught with uncertainties, and demands undivided attention. But, there comes a point where the climber reaches a plateau. Here, she can enjoy the views, take a breather, and reflect on the journey thus far. This plateau represents a stable business. But what if you yearn to reach even greater heights? Then, the next phase of your journey begins: scaling and expansion.

Every ambitious entrepreneur dreams of growth, of seeing her brainchild flourish and extend its branches in multiple directions. While starting a business is a mammoth task in itself, scaling it up is a whole different ball game. It requires not just hard work, but a combination of strategic thinking, adaptability, and often, a sprinkle of audacity.

In this chapter, we're diving deep into the exhilarating world of business growth. From knowing the signs that you're ready to expand, to understanding the different avenues of scaling, and the challenges that come with it - consider this your comprehensive guide to taking your business to the next level. The horizon is vast, and the possibilities are endless.

Diving into the depths of financial intelligence and management can often feel like navigating uncharted waters. But armed with the insights from this chapter, you're no longer a novice sailor but a capable captain of your ship.

Understanding cash flows, ROI, investment strategies, and the intricacies of taxes and laws isn't just about avoiding pitfalls. It's about steering your business vessel toward more prosperous horizons, leveraging the winds of knowledge to propel you forward. As women in business, we don't shy away from challenges; we equip ourselves to meet them head-on.

Always remember: Financial acumen isn't about innate ability but learned expertise. Keep educating yourself, seeking advice when needed, and always staying proactive in your approach. Your business's financial health is a testament to your dedication and resilience. Go on and make those numbers work for you, just as you've been doing in every other aspect of your journey.

When and How to Scale

Scaling isn't just about growth; it's about sustainable growth. Diving headfirst without a plan or doing so prematurely can lead to setbacks, or worse, business failure. On the other hand, waiting too long might mean missed opportunities. Thus, recognizing the right time and knowing the methods of scaling are crucial for any entrepreneur.

1. Recognizing the Right Time:
   - Consistent Demand: One of the primary indicators that it might be time to scale is when there's a consistent demand for your product or service. If customers are clamoring for more and you're frequently selling out or maxing out your

service capacity, it's a good sign that there's room for growth.
- Healthy Cash Flow: Before considering expansion, ensure that your cash flow is stable. It's not just about having extra money but about maintaining a steady inflow and outflow, even during lean months.
- Operational Stability: If day-to-day operations run smoothly and you've got a reliable team in place, it might be time to look at growth.
- Market Conditions: External factors, such as favorable market conditions, technological advancements, or regulatory changes that benefit your sector, can present prime opportunities for scaling.

2. Methods of Scaling:
- Diversifying Offerings: One way to scale is by expanding your product or service line. Listen to customer feedback for new ideas, or consider branching into complementary products or services.
- Tapping into New Markets: Whether it's opening in a new location, reaching a different demographic, or even going international, new markets can offer untapped potential.
- Franchising: For businesses with a replicable model, franchising can be a method to grow without the strain of managing every new outlet.
- Acquisitions: Buying out competitors or complementary businesses can provide instant access to their customer base, technologies, and other assets.
- Leveraging Online Platforms: In the digital age, transitioning or expanding into e-commerce can lead to significant growth.
- Investing in Technology: Automation and technology can enhance productivity, enabling you to serve more customers without a proportional increase in costs.

3. Crafting a Scale Strategy:
   - Business Model Review: Revisit your business model. What worked in the initial stages might need tweaks or overhauls for a larger scale.
   - Financial Analysis: Understand the financial implications of scaling. Will you need funding? If so, what type? Debt, equity, venture capital?
   - Infrastructure and Talent: Scaling might mean needing more human resources or enhancing your infrastructure. Plan your hires, training programs, and infrastructure investments in advance.
   - Risk Assessment: With bigger stakes, there are bigger risks. Undertake a comprehensive risk assessment to identify potential pitfalls and strategies to mitigate them.
   - Feedback Mechanisms: As you grow, maintaining the same level of intimacy with customers can be challenging. Implement systems to continuously gather and act on feedback.

Scaling is a journey of its own, a venture into uncharted territories. But armed with the right knowledge, strategies, and a sprinkle of audacity, you're not just journeying into the unknown—you're charting the course for others to follow.

Expansion Strategies: From Franchising to Mergers

The business world is ever-evolving, with numerous paths to achieve growth. Your brand's expansion strategy should mirror your overarching vision, mission, and, of course, the financial and operational capabilities at your disposal. Here's a detailed guide on some of the most effective expansion strategies to propel your venture to the next level.

1. Franchising:
Franchising allows businesses to grow by granting other entrepreneurs the right to replicate their business model in diverse locations or markets. It's a win-win, where the franchisor gains a new revenue stream without the intricacies of daily operations, and the franchisee accesses a proven model and brand reputation.

- Pros: Immediate brand recognition, faster expansion, and shared advertising benefits.
- Cons: Less control over individual outlets and potential for brand inconsistency.

2. Licensing:
Licensing involves selling your brand's name or technology to another firm. This allows them to create products or services under your brand, giving you royalties in return.

- Pros: Additional revenue with low investment, protection through contractual agreements.
- Cons: Possible brand dilution if the licensee doesn't maintain quality.

3. Joint Ventures:
When two businesses decide to pursue a shared aim by pooling resources, it forms a joint venture. It's like a business marriage, with both parties bringing unique strengths to the table.

- Pros: Access to new markets, shared risks, and pooling of expertise and resources.
- Cons: Potential for conflicts, division of profits.

4. Mergers and Acquisitions (M&As):
   - Mergers: When two businesses combine to form one entity. They're usually between companies of equal size and stature.
   - Acquisitions: When one business buys another. The acquired company may operate as a subsidiary or get fully integrated.
   - Pros: Immediate access to new markets and customers, economies of scale, diversification.
   - Cons: High costs, potential culture clashes, complex integration process.

5. Diversification:
This involves adding new products or services that differ from your existing offerings. It's like branching out into a new genre.

   - Pros: Risk distribution, tapping into new customer bases, increased sales channels.
   - Cons: Diversion of focus, potential for brand confusion.

6. E-commerce and Digital Expansion:
In the digital age, taking your business online or enhancing your digital footprint is an expansion strategy that's hard to ignore.

   - Pros: Access to global markets, 24/7 operations, data-driven insights.
   - Cons: Intense competition, dependency on technology.

7. Global Expansion:
Taking your business international can be the ultimate scaling strategy. This can be done through exports, partnerships, or even setting up operations abroad.

- Pros: Diverse revenue streams, brand prestige, economies of scale.
- Cons: Cultural barriers, regulatory challenges, high upfront costs.

Your choice of expansion strategy will ultimately hinge on your business's unique attributes and your personal ambitions. Remember, every big brand you admire today once faced these very crossroads. It's your turn to carve a path that future entrepreneurs will look up to.

International Expansion: Challenges and Opportunities of Going Global

Stepping onto the global stage is both thrilling and daunting. Entering new markets presents boundless opportunities, yet it also surfaces challenges that can feel like navigating uncharted waters. But, remember, every risk carries the potential for immense reward. Here's a comprehensive look at what awaits as you take your brand beyond borders.

Opportunities of Going Global

- Broader Client Base: Tapping into international markets means access to a more extensive customer pool. More customers translate to more sales, thereby amplifying revenues.
- Diversification: Depending on a single market can be risky. By spreading out, you minimize the impact of regional economic downturns on your overall business health.
- Learning from Different Cultures: International markets offer fresh perspectives and innovative approaches. The knowledge and skills gained can benefit your brand immensely, leading to innovative products or more efficient

processes.
- Brand Prestige: A global presence often bestows a brand with an enhanced image and reputation, making your business a recognized name on a worldwide scale.
- Optimized Supply Chain: Access to global markets can mean better sourcing opportunities, leading to cost savings and quality improvements.

Challenges of Going Global

1. Cultural Nuances: Every region has its unique cultural norms, values, and customer behaviors. Misinterpreting these can lead to marketing blunders or product failures.
2. Regulatory Hurdles: Different countries have varying regulations, standards, and compliance needs. Navigating these requires thorough research, local expertise, and sometimes, a fair bit of patience.
3. Language Barriers: Effective communication is key. While English is a global business language, local languages and dialects can't be ignored, especially in marketing and customer service.
4. Currency and Payment Challenges: Fluctuating exchange rates, different preferred payment methods, and varying tax regimes can complicate transactions.
5. Increased Operational Complexity: Managing operations across time zones, hiring and training a diverse workforce, and coordinating with international teams can be challenging.

Mitigating the Challenges

- Local Partnerships: Collaborate with local businesses or experts who understand the market intricacies and can guide your entry strategy.

- Continuous Research: Stay updated on local consumer trends, regulations, and economic conditions. An informed decision is often a successful one.
- Cultural Sensitivity Training: Equip your team with the knowledge and tools to respect and understand local customs and norms.
- Flexible Business Model: Be ready to adapt. What works in one country might not in another. A flexible approach allows for adjustments as per market needs.
- Utilize Technology: Use tech tools for seamless communication, efficient operations, and real-time monitoring of international ventures.

International expansion is a big leap, but it's one that can redefine your brand's journey. It's like embarking on an epic adventure, filled with unexpected twists and turns but leading to treasures untold. So, gear up, research extensively, forge local alliances, and step into the world with confidence.

Remote Work & Global Teams: Managing and Leveraging a Distributed Team

The workplace has evolved dramatically in recent years. Traditional office setups have transformed, and businesses are leaning more towards harnessing the power of remote work and global teams. There's an undeniable allure to having a team that spans continents, cultures, and time zones. Yet, with these opportunities come unique challenges. Let's delve deep into the world of managing and leveraging a distributed team.

Advantages of Distributed Teams

- Access to Global Talent: No longer are you confined to the talent pool within commuting distance. Now, the world is

your oyster. You can recruit the best from anywhere, leading to a diversified and skilled workforce.
- Cost Savings: Bypassing the traditional office can save on rent, utilities, and other overhead costs. Plus, you might find that talent in certain regions comes at a more budget-friendly rate.
- Increased Productivity: Studies have shown that remote workers often outperform their office-bound counterparts. A comfortable environment, fewer distractions, and the elimination of commuting can bolster efficiency.
- Flexibility: This mode of work can lead to increased job satisfaction, as team members can balance their personal and professional lives more effectively.

Challenges of Distributed Teams

1. Communication Barriers: Without face-to-face interactions, miscommunications can arise. Time zone differences can further complicate synchronous communication.
2. Cultural Differences: Team members from diverse backgrounds might have varying work ethics, communication styles, and expectations.
3. Team Cohesion: Building a sense of unity and camaraderie can be challenging when team members don't meet in person.
4. Security Concerns: Remote work can introduce vulnerabilities if team members access company data from insecure networks or devices.

Strategies for Effective Management

- Robust Communication Tools: Invest in top-tier video conferencing software, instant messaging platforms, and collaborative tools. Regularly scheduled meetings can help

maintain alignment.
- Cultural Awareness Programs: Foster an environment of respect and understanding. Celebrate the diversity of your team and consider training sessions on cultural sensitivity.
- Unified Company Culture: Establish core values, a shared mission, and regular team-building activities. Virtual team-building sessions, like online game nights or trivia, can boost morale.
- Clear Expectations: Set distinct roles, responsibilities, and deliverables. Regular check-ins can help track progress and address any challenges promptly.
- Security Protocols: Ensure all team members are educated on cybersecurity best practices. Consider VPNs, secure collaboration tools, and regular security audits.
- Ongoing Training: As remote work evolves, so do its best practices. Regular training sessions can ensure everyone is on the same page.

In the world of business, embracing remote work and global teams is more than just a trend—it's a transformative shift that, when managed effectively, can lead to unparalleled growth and success. It's like having a symphony orchestra with players from every corner of the world; with the right conductor and harmony, they can produce a masterpiece.

Technology and Scaling: How to Employ Tech to Aid Your Expansion Efforts

As we navigate the complex terrains of business growth, technology emerges as both a facilitator and a game-changer. In our rapidly evolving digital age, the right tech solutions can fuel expansion, streamline operations, and enable us to reach clientele in ways we never thought possible. Let's embark on an enlightening journey, uncovering how technology can be our most trusted ally in scaling efforts.

Benefits of Leveraging Technology for Expansion

1. Operational Efficiency: Automated systems can handle repetitive tasks, freeing up your team to focus on innovation and strategy. Think about tasks like inventory management, customer relationship management, or financial tracking; technology can streamline them all.
2. Data-Driven Decision Making: Advanced analytics tools allow you to glean insights from vast swathes of data. This means more informed decisions and strategies tailored to your unique audience.
3. Global Reach: With digital platforms and e-commerce solutions, your products or services can touch corners of the world you hadn't considered.
4. Personalization at Scale: AI-driven solutions can tailor user experiences, making your clientele feel seen and understood, even as your customer base grows exponentially.
5. Continuous Availability: Chatbots, for example, can provide 24/7 customer support, ensuring clients always have an avenue for queries or assistance.

Key Technologies to Consider

- Cloud Computing: Whether it's data storage or using software-as-a-service (SaaS) tools, the cloud provides scalability without massive upfront infrastructure costs.
- E-commerce Platforms: Solutions like Shopify or WooCommerce can simplify the process of selling globally.
- AI and Machine Learning: These can analyze customer behavior, optimize logistics, or even assist in product

development.
- Collaboration Tools: Platforms like Slack or Trello can keep your expanding team aligned and foster a culture of collaboration, no matter where they're located.
- ERP Systems: Enterprise Resource Planning systems can integrate various business processes into a unified system, ensuring smooth operations as you scale.

Navigating Potential Tech Pitfalls

1. Invest Wisely: It's easy to get wooed by the latest tech solution, but always align investments with clear business objectives.
2. Training: Ensure your team is well-acquainted with any new tools or platforms. An advanced system is only as good as the people using it.
3. Cybersecurity: Expansion often comes with increased security threats. Regular audits, secure systems, and employee training are paramount.
4. Scalability: Opt for tech solutions that can grow with you. The needs of a 10-person team will differ vastly from a 1000-person operation.

In essence, the synergy between your expansion goals and technological tools is paramount for modern success. Think of technology as the wind behind the sails of your expansion ship, propelling you forward into uncharted waters with confidence and precision. Just as a craftsman is only as good as her tools, an entrepreneur's success in scaling is deeply intertwined with the technology she employs.

As we close this chapter on scaling and expansion, it's essential to reflect on our journey.

We've unpacked determining the right time to scale, ventured into the vast terrains of international expansion, and navigated the complex waters of technology in aiding growth. Every aspect, be it remote teams or mergers, plays a vital role in sketching the larger picture of business evolution.

Expanding a business is much like nurturing a tree. It begins as a sapling, needs the right conditions to grow, and over time, with care, blossoms into a magnificent entity, branching out in directions we might never have envisioned at the outset. And while the journey might be riddled with challenges and moments of uncertainty, the fruits of perseverance, informed strategy, and adaptability are immensely rewarding.

Always remember, the world is vast, filled with countless opportunities waiting for the taking. As women entrepreneurs, our vision, resilience, and passion are unmatched. When paired with the right strategies and insights, there's no limit to the heights we can reach.

So, as you gear up to scale those lofty peaks of business growth, always trust in your journey, embrace learning at every juncture, and know that every step, no matter how small, is a leap towards your grand vision.

CHAPTER 10:

Overcoming Adversity

Life, in all its unpredictability, sometimes presents us with tumultuous storms and towering barriers. It's as if the universe is testing our mettle, seeing if we're truly committed to our dreams. Every entrepreneur, regardless of their industry or ambition, faces adversity. It's an unavoidable element of our journeys. But here's the silver lining – adversity, no matter how daunting, often carries the seeds of growth, transformation, and profound learning.

For us women, adversity takes on a unique flavor. It's not just about business challenges, but also the societal expectations, balancing myriad roles, and the occasional self-doubt that creeps in on quiet nights. But if history has shown us anything, it's that women have an unparalleled ability to rise from the ashes, stronger, fiercer, and more determined.

In this chapter, we'll delve deep into the trials and tribulations faced by many female entrepreneurs. We'll uncover strategies to navigate these rough patches and transform challenges into catalysts for growth. Remember, it's not about avoiding the storm, but learning to dance in the rain.

Adversity Women Entrepreneurs Can Potentially Face

Being a woman in the business world comes with a unique set of challenges. While strides have been made towards gender equality, women entrepreneurs often find themselves navigating a labyrinth of issues that their male counterparts might not necessarily encounter. Understanding these adversities is the first step in addressing and overcoming them. Here's a glimpse into some of the common obstacles faced by women entrepreneurs:

- Unequal Access to Funding: Studies have consistently shown that women-led startups receive less venture capital funding compared to those helmed by men. This discrepancy can hamstring the growth of women-founded enterprises right from the outset.
- Gender Stereotypes: Many women entrepreneurs find themselves combating prevailing stereotypes. Whether it's being perceived as too emotional or not assertive enough, these baseless assumptions can hinder decision-making processes and influence external business relationships.
- Balancing Business and Family Life: While societal norms are shifting, women are often still seen as the primary caregivers in families. Juggling the responsibilities of home and business can stretch even the most resilient individual thin.
- Limited Representation in Male-Dominated Industries: Breaking into industries where men have traditionally held the reins, such as tech or finance, can be daunting. It's not just about securing a seat at the table but also ensuring one's voice is heard and respected.
- Wage Gaps: Even as entrepreneurs, women can face disparities in income levels when compared to their male peers in similar ventures.

This gap can affect the overall financial health of their business.
- Network Limitations: Business networks can be largely male-centric, making it harder for women entrepreneurs to establish connections, find mentors, or access business opportunities.
- Navigating Harassment: Sadly, many women in business have encountered instances of harassment or inappropriate behavior. Addressing it without backlash or being dubbed "difficult" can be a tightrope walk.
- Underestimation by Peers: Often, women entrepreneurs might find their ideas or strategies downplayed or attributed to luck rather than business acumen or hard work.
- Lack of Role Models: With fewer women in high-ranking business positions, emerging female entrepreneurs might struggle to find relatable mentors or role models to guide them.
- Cultural and Societal Barriers: In certain cultures, the very idea of women in prominent business roles can be met with resistance. This can add an extra layer of complexity for women entrepreneurs trying to break barriers not just in business but also within their communities.

Navigating these adversities requires a cocktail of grit, intelligence, and resilience. But take heart — challenges often mold incredible leaders. With each hurdle jumped, you're not just paving the way for your success but also trailblazing for the next generation of women entrepreneurs.

Resilience-Building Techniques

The heart of an entrepreneur beats with passion, purpose, and tenacity. Yet, it's the quality of resilience that often distinguishes those who can weather the storms from those who capitulate under pressure. Resilience isn't just a buzzword; it's the very fabric that can mend our spirit in trying times. For women, especially, harnessing this trait can be a game-changer in both business and life.

- Embrace a Growth Mindset: Coined by psychologist Carol Dweck, a growth mindset is the belief that abilities and intelligence can be developed through dedication and hard work. Instead of seeing challenges as insurmountable problems, view them as opportunities to grow and learn.
- Prioritize Self-Care: Resilience isn't about pushing through burnout. Listen to your body and mind. Meditation, exercise, hobbies, or even a simple quiet moment with a cup of tea can reinvigorate your spirit.
- Seek Support: Even the most independent of us need a shoulder to lean on sometimes. Cultivate a support system, whether it's friends, family, or mentor groups. Their perspectives and encouragement can be invaluable.
- Reframe Failures: Instead of seeing setbacks as failures, view them as feedback. Each challenge provides valuable lessons that can shape your next steps.
- Visualize Success: When facing adversity, close your eyes and imagine overcoming it. Visualization not only provides motivation but also paves a mental path towards solutions.
- Educate Yourself: Knowledge is a powerful tool. Equip yourself with the tools, courses, and reading material pertinent to the challenges you're facing. Being informed can demystify issues and offer solutions.
- Develop a Ritual: Having a ritual, whether it's morning journaling or a nightly reflection, can provide stability during turbulent times. This consistency offers a sense of control and predictability.

- Celebrate Small Wins: While it's essential to keep an eye on the larger goal, celebrating minor milestones can provide the much-needed motivation to keep pushing forward.
- Stay Flexible: Being rigid in plans or expectations can lead to added frustration. Adopting a flexible approach allows you to pivot and adapt, making the journey smoother.
- Limit Exposure to Negativity: Surrounding yourself with positive influences and limiting exposure to unnecessary negativity (be it people, news, or other media) can maintain a hopeful perspective.

Remember that resilience is like a muscle. The more you flex it, the stronger it becomes. By incorporating these techniques into your daily life, not only will you be prepared to face adversity head-on, but you'll thrive in its wake, turning stumbling blocks into stepping stones.

Adapting to Unseen Challenges: Dealing with Sudden Market Shifts and Global Events

In the dynamic landscape of business, no amount of planning can predict every curveball that comes your way. From economic recessions to unforeseen global events like pandemics, sudden market shifts can test the mettle of even the most seasoned entrepreneurs. So, how do women entrepreneurs prepare for and adapt to these unpredictable challenges? Let's break it down.

1. Cultivate a Flexible Business Model:
Lean Agility: Embrace a lean business model, which is centered on efficiency, adaptability, and customer feedback. This way, when external circumstances change, you're in a better position to pivot.

Scenario Planning: While you can't predict the future, you can run hypothetical scenarios. Analyze how various situations, from best-case to worst-case, could impact your operations and map out potential responses.

2. Stay Informed:
Market Analysis: Keep your finger on the pulse of global and local market trends. Use tools like Google Trends, industry reports, and market analysis publications to stay informed.

Regular Financial Check-ins: Make it a practice to review your business finances regularly. Understand where you can tighten the belt, and which areas need further investment to weather uncertain times.

3. Strengthen Your Supply Chain:
Diversify Suppliers: Avoid relying on a single supplier. By diversifying your supplier base, you're less vulnerable to disruptions.

Regular Communication: Maintain open channels of communication with suppliers and vendors. In challenging times, collaboration can lead to innovative solutions to common problems.

4. Maintain a Robust Digital Presence:
In a world where physical operations can be disrupted, having a strong online foothold can be a saving grace. Make sure you're leveraging e-commerce, digital marketing, and online networking to its fullest potential.

5. Prioritize Liquidity:
Ensure you have a sufficient cash reserve to handle short-term operational costs. This buffer can be a lifesaver when revenue

streams become unpredictable.

6. Foster a Resilient Team Culture:
The emotional and mental well-being of your team is crucial. Cultivate a culture of transparency, open dialogue, and mutual support. When challenges arise, a cohesive team can be your most significant asset.

7. Revisit and Revise:
Your business plan isn't set in stone. As the market landscape changes, be prepared to revisit your strategies, revise your goals, and recalibrate your approach.

8. Leverage Technology:
Embrace technologies that facilitate remote work, improve communication, and enhance efficiency. Tools like project management software, video conferencing platforms, and cloud storage can be invaluable during disruptions.

9. Engage with Your Community:
Your customers, partners, and broader community are valuable resources. Engage with them to understand their needs, fears, and expectations. This can guide your adaptations and foster loyalty.

10. Embrace Lifelong Learning:
Lastly, view challenges as opportunities for growth. Attend workshops, webinars, and courses that can equip you with new skills and insights. The more you learn, the better prepared you'll be for the next unexpected turn.

While the waters of entrepreneurship are seldom calm, the storms they bring can fortify your ship, making it more resilient and robust for future voyages. With adaptability, foresight, and a pinch of audacity, you can navigate even the most turbulent of times with grace and determination.

Public Relations Crisis Management: Keeping Your Brand's Reputation Intact

Navigating the business realm isn't just about strategy, financial smarts, and building connections. It's also about image and reputation. There may come a time when, despite your best intentions and due diligence, your brand finds itself in the spotlight for the wrong reasons. When that happens, how you manage the situation can either elevate your brand or harm it further. Here's your guide to managing a public relations crisis effectively.

1. Swift and Transparent Communication:
When a crisis hits, it's human nature for people to seek out information. Respond promptly. A timely response shows you're in control and can prevent misinformation from spreading.

2. Understand the Issue Fully:
Before making a statement, ensure you fully understand the depth and breadth of the issue. Gather all the facts, consult with internal teams, and if necessary, with external experts.

3. Take Accountability:
If there was an oversight or mistake on your part, own up to it. Taking responsibility can go a long way in rebuilding trust. Avoid placing blame unless it's genuinely warranted, and even then, approach the situation tactfully.

4. Develop a Comprehensive Action Plan:
Show that you're proactive in addressing the issue. Whether it's a product recall, an apology, or a strategic shift, lay out clear steps on how you're addressing the problem at hand.

5. Keep Internal Teams in the Loop:
Your employees are your brand ambassadors. Keep them informed, provide them with a unified message, and offer guidance on how to handle external queries or concerns.

6. Engage with the Media Smartly:
Depending on the situation, you might need to host a press conference, issue a press release, or grant interviews. Choose a spokesperson who's articulate and calm under pressure. Prepare them with key messages and potential Q&A scenarios.

7. Monitor the Situation:
Use tools to monitor media coverage, social media mentions, and other digital footprints related to the crisis. Understand public sentiment and adjust your strategy accordingly.

8. Learn and Adapt:
Post-crisis, conduct an internal review. What caused the situation? How can you prevent it in the future? Implement changes based on your findings.

9. Rebuild and Reinforce Trust:
Once the immediate crisis subsides, focus on rebuilding trust. This could mean ramping up community engagement, offering special initiatives, or merely continuing to be transparent about changes you've made.

10. Seek External Counsel:
Sometimes, it's beneficial to bring in a third-party expert or PR

firm to help manage the situation, especially if it's particularly delicate or extensive.

Remember, in today's digital age, news travels fast, but so does appreciation for genuine efforts to rectify mistakes. In facing a PR crisis, your goal isn't just damage control, but also showcasing your brand's character and values. It's an opportunity—a challenging one, indeed—to display integrity, leadership, and commitment to your community and customers.

Every entrepreneur's journey is sprinkled with tales of challenges, missed opportunities, and yes, outright failures. But here's the twist: the most remarkable stories often emerge from these very setbacks.

CHAPTER 11:
Power of Continuous Learning

In the fast-paced world of business, there's a constant – change. Markets evolve, technologies advance, and consumer behaviors shift. And while adaptability is essential, there's an underlying force that truly empowers one to ride these waves of change: continuous learning.

Imagine a toolbox. At the start of your entrepreneurial journey, you might have a few essential tools – your initial knowledge, your unique skills, perhaps a sprinkle of instinct. But as you progress, you'll encounter tasks and challenges that your current tools aren't equipped for. Here's where continuous learning becomes your game-changer. With every new skill or knowledge you acquire, you add a tool to your kit, preparing yourself for varied challenges and unlocking new opportunities.

Now, consider this. The world's most successful individuals, from tech magnates to renowned artists, swear by one common practice: they never stop learning. They devour books, attend seminars, engage in workshops, and seek mentorship. They understand that no matter how high they climb, there's always a new horizon to explore, a new boundary to push.

As we delve into this chapter, we'll unearth the immense value of lifelong education, explore avenues for personal and professional growth, and understand how an insatiable curiosity can become one of your strongest assets. Ready to dive deep into the world of continuous learning? Let's embark on this enlightening journey.

"Know thyself," proclaimed the ancient Greek aphorism. But knowing oneself is not a one-time task; it's an ongoing process. Lifelong education is that very pursuit – not just of external knowledge but of a deeper understanding of oneself, one's passions, potentials, and the ever-changing world around.

1. Personal Growth and Evolution:

Every piece of knowledge we acquire or skill we hone doesn't just add to our repertoire; it transforms us. With every book, seminar, or workshop, we become a newer version of ourselves, better equipped to navigate the complexities of our careers and personal lives. It's akin to leveling up in a game, where each level brings its own challenges but also its rewards.

2. Adapting to the Fluid Business Landscape:

In business, stasis can be lethal. What worked a year ago might be obsolete today. Continuous education ensures that we stay updated, be it the latest digital marketing trends, breakthroughs in AI, or shifts in consumer behavior. By being perpetual students, we ensure that we're not just reacting to the world but actively shaping our destiny within it.

3. Networking through Learning:

Courses, seminars, workshops, and even online forums can be goldmines for networking. By being part of a learning community, you're not just gaining knowledge but also building relationships that could be pivotal for your business's growth.

4. Cultivating Curiosity:

Remember when you were a child, and everything was a wonder? That innate curiosity is one of the most potent tools for an entrepreneur. When you continuously learn, you feed that curiosity, ensuring that your approach to business and life remains fresh, innovative, and vivacious.

5. Building Mental Resilience:

Challenging yourself with new learning experiences, stepping out of your comfort zone, and facing the occasional academic failure can also bolster your mental strength. Just as muscles grow through resistance, so does the mind.

6. Expanding Horizons Beyond Business:

Continuous learning isn't just about professional growth. Whether it's picking up a new language, delving into the mysteries of ancient civilizations, or mastering a musical instrument, these pursuits enrich our lives, provide relaxation, and even offer fresh perspectives that can be applied to our businesses.

In essence, the journey of lifelong education is like sailing on an infinite ocean. Each wave brings its challenges, but each horizon offers a new world of possibilities. As women in business, by embracing this voyage, we don't just enhance our enterprises; we elevate ourselves.

Staying Ahead of the Curve: Tuning into Industry Oscillations

The business world is akin to an ever-shifting kaleidoscope. Colors change, patterns evolve, and what's in focus today may blur tomorrow. Especially in today's accelerated age, industry trends can shift with lightning speed. The key to enduring success? Stay inquisitive, stay informed, and most importantly, stay ahead. Here's how to do just that:

- Dedicated Research Time: Schedule a set time in your week – even if it's just an hour – solely dedicated to researching your industry. Peruse articles, watch related webinars, or listen to podcasts. This routine ensures that you're regularly updated and not caught off-guard by sudden shifts.
- Industry-specific Publications and Newsletters: Subscribe to leading journals, magazines, or digital newsletters in your domain. They often feature insights from industry leaders, reviews of the latest tools and techniques, and forecasts that can be invaluable for your business strategy.
- Attend Trade Shows and Conferences: These events are treasure troves of information. They not only showcase the latest innovations but also provide opportunities to gauge the market mood, understand competitor moves, and even strike potential collaborations.
- Engage in Industry Forums and Groups: Platforms like LinkedIn or niche industry websites often host forums or groups where professionals discuss the latest happenings, share challenges, and offer solutions. Engaging here can provide on-the-ground insights that might not make it to formal publications.

- Continuous Training and Courses: Consider enrolling in courses that offer training on the latest tools, technologies, or methodologies in your industry. Platforms like Coursera, Udemy, or industry-specific academies often update their content to reflect the latest trends.
- Network with Peers: Build a solid network of professionals within your industry. Regular interactions, be it casual coffee chats or formal meetings, can provide firsthand information on emerging trends.
- Feedback and Customer Insights: Your customers can be your best informants. Regularly solicit feedback and pay attention to their needs, complaints, and desires. Often, they'll signal a trend before it becomes mainstream.
- Scout the Fringes: Sometimes, the most groundbreaking trends start as fringe movements or niche experiments. Keep an eye on startups, experimental projects, or academic research related to your field.

In a world of constant motion, information is your anchor. By diligently and proactively seeking knowledge, you ensure that instead of being swept away by the tides of change, you ride them, steering your enterprise towards new horizons of success.

Broadening Horizons: The Magic of Diverse Skillsets

The richest tapestries are woven with a myriad of threads, each contributing to a greater, stunning whole. Similarly, an entrepreneur armed with a multifaceted skillset doesn't just survive — they thrive. Venturing beyond your core domain doesn't dilute your expertise. Instead, it adds dimensions, opening doors to innovations and opportunities that a single-track mind might miss.

The Fusion of Fields:
Often, the most groundbreaking innovations occur at the intersection of disciplines. Think of Steve Jobs, who believed that technology alone wasn't enough — it's technology married with liberal arts, married with the humanities, that yields the results we treasure. By diversifying your skillsets, you're essentially building bridges between fields, and it's on these bridges that the magic happens.

Personal Growth and Adaptability:
Diving into unfamiliar terrains enhances cognitive flexibility. You become more adaptable, a trait invaluable in the unpredictable world of business. If one avenue faces a roadblock, a diversified skillset ensures you can pivot and find another route to your goal.

Avenues to Explore:
Digital Literacy: In today's digitized age, understanding the basics of coding, digital marketing, or e-commerce can drastically elevate your business game.
Soft Skills: Communication, leadership, negotiation — these skills, while not tied to a particular domain, can amplify your effectiveness in any field.
Financial Acumen: Even if you aren't in the financial sector, understanding the basics of economics, investment, or even just personal finance can lead to better business decisions.
Design Thinking: This approach to problem-solving and creativity can be applied far beyond product design, offering innovative solutions in any industry.

How to Dive In:
Workshops and Webinars: Bite-sized, focused sessions that provide a quick dive into a new area.

Mentorships: Finding someone experienced in a field you're curious about can provide insights books or courses might miss.
Collaborative Projects: Team up with experts from other domains on joint projects. The hands-on experience is often the best teacher.

While deep expertise in one's core domain is crucial, it's the peripheral vision, the ability to see and connect dots across disciplines, that often marks the difference between a good entrepreneur and a great one. Embrace the mosaic of learning, and watch as your business tapestry becomes richer, more vibrant, and infinitely more impactful.

Networking as Learning: Every Conversation, A Lesson in Disguise

We often view networking as a two-dimensional endeavor: an exchange of business cards, LinkedIn connections, and perhaps a follow-up email or two. But, ladies, it's time we shed this limiting perspective. At its core, networking is a profound learning experience, a dance of insights, perspectives, and shared wisdom. Here's why every handshake and conversation is a masterclass waiting to unravel:

1. Gleaning Industry Knowledge:
Ever sat down with a peer from your industry and realized there's a significant trend you missed? These moments underscore the importance of diverse interactions. Every person you meet has a unique vantage point, a distinct slice of the industry pie. By listening and engaging, you tap into this reservoir of insights.

2. Unpacking Personal Experiences:
Each individual's journey through the business landscape is a story studded with trials, errors, triumphs, and strategies. When someone shares their tale, it's not mere storytelling; it's a lesson. The failures they've encountered, the risks they've taken, and the milestones they've achieved can guide your path.

3. Soft Skills in Action:
Observe a seasoned networker, and you're essentially watching a masterclass in soft skills. Their body language, the way they handle interruptions, how they navigate disagreements — there's a world of knowledge in these subtleties. Take notes, not just on what is said, but how it's conveyed.

4. Diverse Perspectives:
Engaging with people from different backgrounds, cultures, and industries is like opening a window to a myriad of worldviews. It challenges our assumptions, introduces us to new paradigms, and fosters a holistic perspective — invaluable for any entrepreneur aiming for global resonance.

Elevate Your Networking Game:

- Active Listening: It's more than just hearing words. It's about understanding the underlying emotions, motivations, and insights.
- Ask Thoughtful Questions: Move beyond the surface-level "What do you do?" Dive deeper. Ask about challenges faced, trends observed, or lessons learned.
- Share Your Stories Too: Networking is a two-way street. As you learn, contribute your insights to the pool. Your experiences are equally valuable.

- Keep an Open Mind: Sometimes, the most profound lessons come from the most unexpected sources. Be open, receptive, and non-judgmental.

In the grand tapestry of entrepreneurship, networking isn't just a strand; it's the very thread weaving through each aspect, connecting dots, creating patterns, and enriching our professional journey. So, the next time you step into a networking event, see it not just as a room full of potential contacts, but as a library brimming with stories, lessons, and wisdom.

Industry Thought Leaders: Tracing the Footsteps of Women Who Shape Tomorrow

In the ever-evolving world of business and entrepreneurship, staying ahead of the curve often means keeping your ear to the ground, listening intently to the voices that matter. Among these influential voices, a chorus of phenomenal women has emerged, leading the charge, setting trends, and reshaping industries. So, why is it crucial for budding female entrepreneurs to keep tabs on these industry thought leaders? And how can one effectively do it?

The Why:
- Setting the Pace: Women thought leaders often challenge the status quo, pushing boundaries and setting new standards. By observing their trajectory, one can gain insights into the direction the industry might take.
- Relatable Narratives: While universal in many of their strategies and insights, women leaders often navigate a distinct set of challenges tied to gender biases. Their stories and solutions can be particularly enlightening for fellow women in the entrepreneurial space.

- Diverse Perspectives: Women, especially those from varied cultural, racial, and socio-economic backgrounds, bring a plethora of perspectives to the table. Their narratives can introduce you to considerations you hadn't previously contemplated.
- Inspiration Galore: Simply put, witnessing a woman break ceilings and dominate in traditionally male-led spaces is pure fuel for ambition. Their victories become wind beneath your wings.

The How:
- Follow Their Work: This may sound basic, but start by keeping up with their publications, interviews, podcasts, and any other content they produce. Their thoughts, predictions, and analyses can be golden nuggets of information.
- Engage in Discussions: Many thought leaders are active on platforms like LinkedIn or X. Engage with their posts, ask questions, or spark discussions. This active participation will not only increase your knowledge but might also get you noticed.
- Attend Conferences and Webinars: Look out for events where they're speaking. If attending in person isn't feasible, many conferences now offer virtual attendance options.
- Read Their Books: If they've penned a book or been the subject of one, make it a part of your reading list. Books often delve deeper, providing a comprehensive look into their philosophies and methodologies.
- Join Industry Groups: Various professional networks and groups focus on industry-specific discussions. Being part of these can keep you updated about the latest from thought leaders.

CHAPTER 12:

Women in Leadership

In the ever-evolving tapestry of business and society, a vibrant thread stands out, weaving tales of strength, wisdom, and vision. That thread is women in leadership. Their stories aren't just about breaking glass ceilings; they encapsulate a myriad of experiences, challenges, successes, and lessons that offer a fresh perspective on leadership.

Leading with Confidence and Authenticity: A Woman's Guide

As we navigate the challenges of modern workspaces and leadership roles, we find that certain principles become pillars, grounding us and providing direction. Here, we aim to distill essential insights for women striving to cement their place at leadership tables, to assert themselves without hesitation, and to break through ceilings, glass or otherwise.

Embracing Your Seat at the Leadership Table
Historically, women have been underrepresented in leadership roles. It's not due to a lack of capability or ambition but often due to societal conditioning and systemic barriers. But times are changing, and it's crucial for women to claim their rightful place.

Action Steps:
1. Start by asserting yourself in meetings. Speak up, share your ideas, and make your voice heard.
2. Seek projects that are outside your comfort zone. Challenge equals growth.
3. Remember that self-worth isn't about ego. It's about recognizing the value you bring.

Nurturing Growth Through Mentorship
There's a proverb that states, "If you want to go fast, go alone. If you want to go far, go together." Mentorship, both as a mentee and later as a mentor, can pave the way for accelerated personal and professional growth.

Action Steps:
1. Identify industry leaders whose values align with yours.
2. Reach out for guidance, framing it as a learning opportunity.
3. As you advance, pay it forward. Become a mentor to younger women in your industry.

Redefining "Having It All"
The notion of "having it all" has been both an aspiration and a point of contention. It's essential to understand that "all" is subjective. Every woman has her definition of success, and it's crucial to set personal benchmarks.

Action Steps:
1. Take some time to reflect on what success looks like to you.
2. Set boundaries in both personal and professional spheres.
3. Celebrate your milestones, whether they are big or small.

Uplifting and Supporting Fellow Women
As we rise, it's our duty and privilege to lift others. There's immense power in community and collective growth.

Action Steps:
1. Actively engage in or form women-centric professional networks.
2. Share opportunities and resources.
3. Celebrate the achievements of other women as you would your own.

Tackling Workplace Biases Head-On
Biases, whether overt or covert, can hinder growth. Recognizing them is the first step, followed by a strategic approach to counter them.

Action Steps:
1. Equip yourself with knowledge. Understand the most common biases women face in professional settings.
2. Address biases when you encounter them. Sometimes, it's a matter of opening a dialogue.
3. Advocate for diversity and inclusion training in your workplace.

In our pursuit of leadership, it's essential to remain authentic, to lead with both heart and head, and to carve paths that future generations of women can tread more easily. With determination, resilience, and community support, there's no summit too high for us to reach.

A Woman's Guide to Mastering Confidence

Success isn't just about skills or talent; at its heart, there's a pulse of confidence. Especially for women, navigating the labyrinth of self-assuredness comes with its unique challenges and triumphs. In this section, we'll dissect what fuels confidence and give you tools to fan its flames.

The Foundations of Self-Assuredness
Contrary to popular belief, confidence isn't just handed down through DNA. It's molded by experiences, interactions, and introspections. It's a garden waiting to be nurtured.

Reminders & Revelations:
- Revisit moments of accomplishment, big or small. They're testament to what you can achieve.
- Treasure feedback, especially the kind that nudges you to grow.
- Cultivate a circle that roots for you, energizes you, and believes in you.

Venturing Out & Amplifying Courage
Dive into the unknown not with the certainty of success, but with the valor to face potential failure. These leaps of faith magnify confidence.

Ways to Venture:
- Start with baby steps. Opt for challenges slightly off your beaten path.
- See failure as a mentor, not a monster. There's wisdom in every stumble.
- Chronicle your strides; let them be a reminder of how far you've come.

Escaping the Web of Perfection Perfection, often a mirage, can be an anchor weighing down confidence. Break free by seeking excellence, not flawlessness.

Paths to Progress:
- Adopt the credo: "Progress over perfection."
- Set achievable goals. Celebrate when they're met, and recalibrate when they're not.
- Relish the journey. Each step, backward or forward, is a part of your story.

Harboring a Growth-Centric Outlook
Switch gears from a static viewpoint to one that's all about evolution. Challenges transform into chances, and setbacks become setups.

Growth Goals:
- Foster a thirst for learning. Dive into the 'why' and 'how' of things.
- Shift perspectives; see hurdles as growth spurts waiting to happen.
- Welcome feedback with open arms and an open mind.

The Authenticity-Courage Connection
Real confidence doesn't wear masks. It thrives on authenticity, embraces quirks, and dances to its own rhythm.

Embracing Authenticity:
- Indulge in introspection. Recognize your strengths, and acknowledge your passions.
- Affirm your worth, independent of accolades and applause.
- Let your authentic spirit shine, even when the surroundings seem dim.

Confidence isn't a monolith; it's an ever-evolving entity. With conscious efforts, unwavering self-belief, and a tribe that uplifts, women can harness its power, making it a guiding light in all endeavors.

Stepping Into Vulnerability: Our Catalyst for Growth

At the heart of our life's expedition, beyond the layers of defenses, skills, and intellect, lies vulnerability. This chapter paints the landscape of vulnerability, demonstrating how it is not just an emotional state but a transformative one.

Decoding Vulnerability:

Peeling back the layers, vulnerability stands tall, not as a sign of fragility, but as a testament to courage.
- Fact vs Fiction:

Vulnerability transcends mere exposure. It's about presenting our true selves, untouched by facades.
- The Power in Raw Reality:

Vulnerability doesn't mean unveiling every secret; it's about an honest self-presentation, in its pure form.

Turning Tables: From Shame to Empowerment:

While shame has its talons deep, vulnerability, when harnessed, can shift us from a place of stagnation to empowerment.
- Building Resilience:

Pinpoint what fuels feelings of inadequacy. Using vulnerability as a compass, rewrite the narrative from 'lacking' to 'abundance.'

Building Bridges through Authenticity:

True connections are born when we allow ourselves to be seen, fully, without reservations.
- Cultivating Connections:

Being there, wholly, speaks louder than words. It's less

about solving and more about resonating.
- Honoring Boundaries:

Openness has its virtues, but vulnerability values discretion over full disclosure.

Living Out Loud:

Embracing every facet of life, from highs to lows, is the essence of a life lived vulnerably.
- Moments of Elevation:

Indulge in soulful ventures, fostering moments that echo with joy and thankfulness.
- Embracing Imperfections:

Imperfections aren't blemishes; they're stamps of uniqueness, shaping our narrative.

Innovation through Openness:

Vulnerability can be the birthplace of unparalleled creativity. It's when we're most exposed that we often birth brilliance.
- Venturing into the Void:

The unfamiliar isn't intimidating; it's a canvas waiting for a masterpiece.
- Valuing the Voyage:

It's often the journey, peppered with trials and triumphs, that holds more value than the endpoint.

In this exploration, we learn vulnerability is not about weakness but about transformation. Allowing ourselves to be truly visible, in our glory and our imperfections, paves the way for genuine connections, inspiring creativity, and unshakable courage.

As we stand on the precipice of a new era, it's invigorating to witness the ascent of women in leadership roles, a panorama that paints a mosaic of strength, innovation, and resilience. Yet, leadership isn't merely about titles or positions; it's about influence, impact, and the ability to evoke change.

Women, with their multifaceted experiences, bring to the table a unique blend of empathy, decisiveness, and vision. Their stories aren't just tales of success, but sagas of overcoming systemic barriers, challenging age-old norms, and rewriting narratives.

While the path has been arduous, the trajectory is clear: women are not just participants in leadership; they are shaping its very essence. As we've traversed through this chapter, from the nuances of confidence to the transformative power of vulnerability, we've unearthed the myriad facets of women in command.

However, leadership is a journey, not a destination. It demands continuous learning, adaptation, and the audacity to challenge the status quo. For all the budding women leaders reading this, know that your journey will be unique, but the collective legacy you leave behind will echo in the annals of history.

CHAPTER 13:
AI For Business

Ladies, it's time to pull up a chair to one of the most transformative tables of our era: Artificial Intelligence in Business. As we stand at the precipice of a technological revolution, the landscape of business is evolving in ways that were once the stuff of science fiction. And guess what? Women are not just active participants but are leading this charge, bringing unique perspectives, creativity, and finesse to this brave new world.

But why is AI becoming the buzzword in boardrooms? It's not just about robots or high-tech companies. It's about harnessing an intelligent toolset to make smarter decisions, anticipate market shifts, and provide unparalleled customer experiences. Whether you're an entrepreneur carving out a niche in the market or an executive in a global conglomerate, understanding AI is no longer optional; it's essential.

This chapter isn't just a guide to AI's intricacies. It's a celebration of women pioneers, innovators, and trailblazers who are leveraging AI to shape the future. We'll uncover the basics, delve into its applications, and discuss the ethical considerations unique to AI—all while highlighting the monumental contributions of women.

The Origin Story: Tracing the Path of AI

The narrative of artificial intelligence might seem like it belongs to the 21st century, but the seeds were sown much earlier. It all began in the mid-20th century, with the dream of creating machines that could mimic human intelligence. The term "Artificial Intelligence" was officially coined in 1956, marking the start of an endeavor to push computational limits.

Throughout the 20th century, there were waves of optimism followed by "AI winters"—periods of skepticism and reduced funding. However, the dream persisted, and with advances in technology and data availability, AI began to find its footing in various business realms in the 21st century.

AI, Machine Learning, Deep Learning: The Trinity of Modern Business Tech

While many use these terms interchangeably, they represent layers of a complex pyramid.
- Artificial Intelligence (AI): At its core, AI is the overarching concept of machines being able to carry out tasks in ways that we consider "smart". It's a broad field that encompasses everything from robotic process automation to actual robotics.
- Machine Learning (ML): This is a subset of AI. Here, we feed machines data and let them learn on their own. Think of it as teaching computers to learn from experience. The more data you give, the better they become.
- Deep Learning: Deep within the layers of ML lies deep learning. It's a subset of ML that uses neural networks with many layers (hence "deep"). It's been a game-changer for tasks like image and speech recognition.

AI in the Business Tapestry: Then and Now

Historically, businesses have been quick to adopt innovations, and AI was no different. The earliest business applications of AI were in databases and basic automation. But, as the technology advanced, so did its potential. Today, AI impacts everything—from marketing with personalized customer experiences to supply chain optimizations, fraud detection, and beyond.

For the modern woman in business, understanding AI is akin to understanding the pulse of the market. It's no longer a sci-fi dream, but a tangible tool that, when wielded right, can set you leagues apart from the competition.

In essence, AI is the silent engine powering many aspects of modern businesses. As we delve deeper into this chapter, we'll understand not just its mechanics, but also its potential to revolutionize industries, with women leaders at the helm.

AI: The Modern Business Catalyst

In today's competitive business landscape, it's not just about keeping pace—it's about setting the pace. With AI, businesses can optimize operations, reduce overheads, and deliver unparalleled service. Let's consider this: A process that once took hours of human input can now be streamlined in mere seconds, with even more precision.

1. Redefining the Supply Chain:
The logistics and supply chain sector has long been a maze of complexity. Enter AI, and the labyrinth becomes a lot more navigable.

- Predictive Analysis: AI can forecast demand, ensuring businesses have just the right amount of stock. Overstocking and stockouts? They're becoming concerns of the past.
- Smart Logistics: From route optimization for delivery trucks to real-time shipment tracking, AI is revolutionizing the logistics domain, ensuring timely deliveries and efficient operations.

2. HR and AI: Perfect Partners:
The HR department, often swamped with applications and administrative tasks, finds a reliable ally in AI.
- Resume Screening: AI-powered tools can swiftly sift through hundreds of applications, shortlisting candidates based on parameters set by the company, all while eliminating human biases.
- Employee Engagement and Well-being: Some AI tools can analyze employee feedback and concerns in real-time, aiding HR in crafting better work policies and environments.

3. Elevating Customer Service with AI:
The modern consumer expects swift, efficient, and personalized service. AI is the silent workforce meeting these expectations.
- Chatbots and Virtual Assistants: Be it answering queries, booking appointments, or troubleshooting, AI-driven chatbots are providing 24/7 customer support.
- Personalized Experience: AI algorithms can analyze consumer behavior and preferences, curating tailored product recommendations and advertisements.

Tools and Platforms Elevating AI Integration:

To seamlessly integrate AI into business operations, various tools and platforms are available, catering to different needs.

- IBM Watson: A robust platform offering AI solutions for various sectors, from healthcare to finance.
- Google Cloud AI: Offers machine learning services and tools that can enhance applications with sight, language, conversation, and structured data.
- HubSpot: While primarily a marketing tool, its AI features help in content recommendations, lead scoring, and chatbots, to name a few.

Navigating the Data Deluge

In this digital era, every click, every transaction, every interaction generates data. But raw data, as vast and overwhelming as it can be, is just noise until it's interpreted, analyzed, and transformed into actionable intelligence. This is where AI swoops in, becoming the bridge between colossal data streams and strategic decision-making.

Cracking the Code: AI's Interpretation of Big Data

Modern businesses generate data at an astonishing rate. AI, with its machine learning capabilities, can sift through these mountains of data, discern patterns, and produce insights that would be nearly impossible for human analysts to achieve in real time.

- Natural Language Processing (NLP): AI can analyze textual data, be it customer reviews or feedback, extracting sentiments and gauging overall customer satisfaction or

areas of concern.
- Image Recognition: From scanning social media posts to analyzing satellite images for agricultural patterns, AI-powered image recognition is reshaping industries.

Predictive Analytics: Gazing into the Business Crystal Ball

Predictive analytics is more than a buzzword—it's a transformative tool that allows businesses to anticipate market trends, customer behaviors, and potential challenges.

- Sales and Demand Forecasting: By analyzing past sales data and current market trends, AI can predict future sales with remarkable accuracy, enabling businesses to streamline inventory management and optimize production.
- Risk Management: Financial institutions utilize AI to assess loan and credit risks, analyzing potential borrowers' data to predict the likelihood of default.
- Customer Retention: By evaluating customer interaction data, AI can identify signs of potential customer churn, allowing businesses to implement retention strategies proactively.

Strategic Formation Through AI Insights

Equipped with predictive insights, business leaders can form strategies that are not just reactive but proactive. It's the difference between responding to market shifts and anticipating them.

- Product Development: By gauging customer feedback and analyzing market needs, companies can harness AI to develop products that resonate with market demand.

- Marketing and Campaign Strategy: AI can predict which marketing strategies will resonate most with target demographics, maximizing ROI on marketing spends.

In essence, AI's role in data-driven decision-making is akin to a seasoned guide helping women business leaders traverse the vast landscape of the corporate realm. It's not about making decisions for them but equipping them with the insights, foresights, and tools necessary to make informed, strategic choices. And as these decisions shape the future of industries, the role of AI as an invaluable ally becomes undeniably clear.

A New Age Toolset

The advancement of AI is not a promise of the future—it's a reality of the present. For women entrepreneurs ready to embrace this digital evolution, the horizon is teeming with tools designed to streamline operations, enhance customer engagement, and foster growth. Let's get into the nitty-gritty of some of the most accessible and transformative AI applications available to women in business today.

1. Chatbots: Your 24/7 Customer Representative
Ever visited a website and been greeted by a pop-up chat window offering assistance? That's likely a chatbot. Powered by AI, these digital assistants can:
- Answer frequently asked questions.
- Guide users to relevant website sections.
- Provide instant customer support.
- Gather preliminary data for human representatives.

For women-led startups, especially those operating with limited personnel, chatbots can be a cost-effective solution to ensure uninterrupted customer service.

2. Midjourney: Crafting Visual Narratives with AI

Navigating the landscape of stock imagery can be a daunting task, especially when you have a clear visual in mind but can't find the perfect match. Enter Midjourney. This cutting-edge AI responds to verbal cues, generating stock images that align precisely with specified themes or emotions. Imagine articulating a concept, a mood, or even an abstract idea, and then having a platform generate visuals that encapsulate your vision.

For women entrepreneurs in creative industries or those managing brand aesthetics, this means:

- No more hours wasted in searching for the perfect image.
- Ability to create bespoke visuals that resonate with brand messaging.
- Cost-saving on hiring graphic designers for custom images.

Moreover, AI's capabilities don't end with visuals. Present-day AI tools also enable users to:

- Compose digital music based on mood or genre preferences, offering tailor-made soundtracks for branding efforts.
- Generate scripts for videos, infomercials, or ads, cutting down on content creation time and ensuring brand coherence.
- Design graphics and layouts, from website UI to promotional materials, guided by AI insights on user engagement and aesthetic appeal.

3. Automated Social Media Marketing

Social media is a pivotal space for brand visibility. AI-driven tools can:

- Schedule posts for optimal engagement times.
- Analyze user engagement to refine marketing strategies.
- Predict content trends, ensuring your brand remains

relevant.

4. Smart Inventory Management
For businesses dealing in tangible goods, inventory management can be a logistical challenge. AI can:
- Predict stock requirements based on sales trends.
- Optimize storage solutions.
- Alert businesses to replenish stocks, preventing out-of-stock situations.

5. Financial Forecasting
Cash flow predictions, budgeting, and financial forecasting can be significantly enhanced using AI tools. By analyzing past financial data, these tools offer:
- Accurate sales revenue predictions.
- Expense forecasting.
- Insights into potential financial challenges.

6. HR & Recruitment Enhancements
AI tools can streamline the hiring process by:
- Scanning resumes for relevant keywords.
- Predicting candidate suitability based on data analytics.
- Scheduling interviews and sending automated follow-ups.

To the women entrepreneurs of today: AI is more than just a tech buzzword; it's an ally, a toolset, and a game-changer. Integrating AI into your business processes isn't about replacing the human touch—it's about enhancing it, making businesses more efficient, customer-centric, and adaptive to the ever-evolving market dynamics. Embrace it, and watch your entrepreneurial journey transform.

Walking the Tightrope of Tech and Ethics

As AI becomes an indispensable part of business infrastructures, the ethical concerns surrounding its deployment can't be overlooked. For women entrepreneurs, who often lead with empathy and a keen sense of social responsibility, navigating this new territory involves a blend of technical know-how and moral compass alignment.

1. The Unbiased Algorithm Fallacy
Contrary to popular belief, algorithms aren't innately impartial. They are crafted by humans, and thus, can inherit biases. When fed data tainted by historical prejudices, the AI models can perpetuate those very biases, leading to skewed results. In realms like recruitment or customer targeting, this can be particularly problematic, fostering discriminatory practices.

Actionable Steps:
- Ensure data sets are diverse, encompassing a broad spectrum of variables.
- Periodically review AI decisions to detect and rectify any discernible patterns of bias.
- Engage in 'ethical AI' workshops and seminars to stay informed about best practices.

2. The Automation Paradox
The allure of automation is undeniable. Efficiency, consistency, and scalability are but a few benefits. However, there's a flip side. Over-reliance on automation can jeopardize human jobs, and sometimes, the human touch is irreplaceable in decision-making, where intuition and experiential wisdom play pivotal roles.

Actionable Insights:
- Strive for a symbiotic relationship between AI and human workforce. Let machines handle data-heavy tasks, while humans focus on strategy and intuition-based roles.
- Offer upskilling programs for employees, enabling them to navigate and manage AI tools, rather than being replaced by them.
- Recognize and celebrate the irreplaceable facets of human contribution, ensuring a harmonious blend of tech and touch.

3. AI's Uncharted Territories
With AI's rapid advancements, we're often venturing into uncharted territories, where traditional ethics might not offer clear guidance. Questions about data privacy, consent, and transparency often arise.

Steps to Steer Clear:
- Always prioritize user consent. Before deploying any AI tool that interacts with user data, ensure transparency and secure permission.
- Implement stringent data protection protocols, reassuring clients and customers about the sanctity of their information.
- Foster a culture of ethical tech adoption within the organization, ensuring every stakeholder understands and respects the boundaries.

For women at the forefront of businesses, integrating AI is not merely a tech decision but an ethical journey. By anchoring AI's vast possibilities in a bedrock of ethical considerations, we not only optimize our business ventures but also pave the way for a more equitable and conscious entrepreneurial landscape.

Continuous Learning: The Lighthouse in the AI Storm

The velocity at which AI is advancing can sometimes feel overwhelming. Algorithms and systems that were en vogue a year ago might be deemed archaic today. In this whirlwind, the beacon that can guide businesses is continuous learning.

- Commit to Regular Training: Encourage team members to attend workshops, webinars, and courses focused on AI advancements relevant to your industry. Make it a company culture staple.
- In-House Think Tanks: Create teams or groups within your organization dedicated to understanding and experimenting with AI. Let them be the catalysts driving innovation from within.
- Collaborate with Academic Institutions: Universities and research institutions are often at the forefront of AI breakthroughs. Forming partnerships can keep businesses updated with the latest in the field.

Strategic Foresight: Paving the Way

To not just survive but thrive in the AI age, businesses need more than just reactive measures. They require proactive strategies that anticipate changes.

- AI Roadmaps: Design a blueprint detailing how AI will be integrated into different facets of the business in the upcoming years. This allows for budgeting, training, and resource allocation to be well-planned.
- Diversified Skill Sets: While specialized skills are invaluable, encouraging cross-domain knowledge can foster creativity. An HR executive with a basic understanding of AI can bring innovative ideas for talent management, for instance.
- Feedback Mechanisms: Ensure that there are channels for feedback from both customers and employees. Their on-

ground experience can offer crucial insights into how AI implementations are faring and where tweaks might be needed.

For women entrepreneurs, the AI-driven future is not a challenge to be feared but an opportunity to be seized. It's a canvas upon which their vision, aided by the brushes of AI tools, can paint masterpieces of innovation, efficiency, and growth. By championing adaptability and maintaining a relentless focus on upskilling, they're not just preparing for this future - they're shaping it.

As we draw the curtain on this exploration of AI in business, one message stands tall: the future of AI is not just about algorithms and codes; it's intrinsically tied to human spirit, intuition, and ambition. For women entrepreneurs charting the waters of this AI revolution, the journey is as much about harnessing the transformative power of technology as it is about fortifying it with the timeless strengths of empathy, vision, and collaboration. Embracing AI doesn't mean relinquishing the human touch; it's about amplifying it. And as women stand at this crossroads of tradition and innovation, they are poised not just to navigate, but to lead, inspire, and redefine the very contours of business success.

CHAPTER 14:

Maintaining Work-Life Balance

In the whirlwind of entrepreneurship, where business goals meet personal aspirations, the teeter-totter of work-life balance often becomes the unsung challenge. It's the 21st century, and "burning the midnight oil" isn't just a poetic idiom anymore. It's the Instagram story of a sleep-deprived start-up founder, the background hum of late-night emails, the Zoom calls that blur into dinner time. But here's the plot twist - it doesn't have to be this way.

For the modern woman, wearing multiple hats - entrepreneur, mother, partner, friend, mentor - the juggle is real. But what if we could turn that juggle into a graceful ballet of balance? Imagine a world where deadlines meet date nights without a glitch, where business conquests coexist with cozy family weekends, and where personal well-being isn't a luxury, but a well-deserved norm. Intrigued? Let's dive into the art and science of mastering that ever-elusive work-life equilibrium, tailored for the woman who's out to have it all.

The Modern Woman's Juggle: Business and Personal Life

The idea of 'having it all' has been around for a while, but what does it genuinely mean in our hyper-connected era?

As we navigate the digital age, the lines between professional pursuits and personal endeavors often blur, creating a web of interlaced responsibilities. For many, a smartphone ping could signal an email from a client, a reminder for a child's virtual school meeting, or a message from a friend in a different time zone. All equally pressing, all demanding immediate attention.

Historically, women have been the choreographers of household harmony, ensuring everything runs smoothly. With the evolution of women in the business landscape, the choreography has grown complex. The dance now includes boardroom meetings, product launches, team check-ins, and yes, ensuring there's milk in the fridge or attending a child's recital. It's like mastering the waltz and hip-hop simultaneously.

What makes this juggle particularly challenging for women is the societal expectations and internalized pressures. A successful business pitch in the morning can be quickly overshadowed by the guilt of missing a family event in the evening. Conversely, a delightful day spent with loved ones might come at the cost of looming work tasks.

But while challenging, this intersection of roles also presents a strength unique to women. It fosters resilience, adaptability, and an uncanny ability to prioritize. Every decision becomes a strategy; every hour, a resource. Recognizing and addressing the challenge is the first step in crafting a life where business and personal spheres not only coexist but complement each other beautifully.

Mental and Emotional Well-being: The Non-Negotiables

We've all been there: that moment when you're staring at your computer screen, lost in a maze of tasks, feeling like you're on the brink of a meltdown. And it's no secret - as dynamic businesswomen, the relentless pace can sometimes feel overwhelming. But here's a golden nugget of wisdom: Just as you wouldn't ignore a glaring glitch in your business plan, you shouldn't overlook the health of your mind and emotions. It's the silent engine behind every successful endeavor.

- Start with Self-awareness: Understand your stressors. Is it a looming deadline, a challenging client, or perhaps the guilt of missing personal commitments? Recognizing what triggers stress or anxiety is the first step in managing it.
- Set Clear Boundaries: This might mean having dedicated 'office hours' at home, taking planned digital detox days, or even setting specific times when you're completely 'off' from work.
- Mindful Moments: Whether it's a deep-breathing exercise during a hectic day, morning meditation, or a midday walk, carving out pockets of mindfulness can be a game-changer. It's like hitting the reset button on your brain.
- Embrace the Power of 'No': As tempting as it might be to accept every opportunity or invitation, sometimes prioritizing well-being means gracefully declining.
- Seek Support: Whether it's a professional therapist, a trusted mentor, or an understanding friend, having someone to talk to can offer clarity. Remember, seeking help isn't a sign of weakness; it's a strategy of the wise.
- Celebrate the Small Wins: Maybe you tackled that challenging task or simply took a well-deserved break. Celebrating these moments elevates your mood and gives perspective.
- Feed Your Mind: Just as you'd nourish your body with wholesome food, ensure your mind is consuming uplifting and enriching content. Books, podcasts, or seminars -

choose sources that resonate and inspire.
- Physical Well-being = Mental Well-being: Exercise isn't just about maintaining a figure; it's a proven booster for mental health. Find an activity you love, be it yoga, dancing, or jogging. Your mind will thank you.
- Embrace Imperfection: The world won't end if there's a minor hiccup in plans or if everything isn't picture-perfect. Allow yourself the grace of being human.

At the heart of it, prioritizing mental and emotional well-being isn't a luxury or an afterthought—it's the foundation. By ensuring you're mentally agile and emotionally resilient, you're not just setting yourself up for success in business, but in the grand, beautiful venture of life.

Automation and Delegation: The Unsung Heroes of Balance

Alright, powerhouse, here's the deal: You have the passion, the ambition, and the brilliance to craft a world-class business, but you've also got just 24 hours in a day (I checked, it's the same for all of us!). So, how do those uber-successful mavens seem to achieve it all while still having time to sip a margarita on a beach somewhere? Enter the dynamic duo of automation and delegation.

Unlocking Automation's Potential:

Automating repetitive tasks doesn't just free up your schedule; it can ensure accuracy and consistency. Tools like Customer Relationship Management (CRM) software, email marketing platforms, and even simple calendar apps can handle tasks without your constant oversight.

- Set It and (Mostly) Forget It: Think about those tasks that have a clear pattern. Billing, newsletter sending, appointment reminders? There's software out there that can manage those on autopilot.
- Stay Updated: As technology evolves, new automation tools continually pop up. Keeping an eye out and being willing to adapt can save countless hours in the long run.

Delegation: Sharing the Load

It's hard letting go, especially when your business feels like your baby. But delegation isn't about shirking responsibilities. It's about trusting others to bring their expertise into your vision.

- Hire for Fit and Skill: When looking to delegate, search for individuals who align with your company's ethos and possess the skills you need. It's a mix of the right attitude and the right aptitude.
- Clear Communication is Key: Make sure your team knows what's expected. Whether it's a detailed brief or regular check-ins, ensure everyone's on the same page.
- Empower and Trust: Provide the necessary training, but once you delegate, resist the urge to micromanage. Trust in your team's abilities.

But Why Does It Matter?

At the core, automation and delegation are about sustainability. They allow you to maintain the stamina and creativity that likely propelled your business in its initial stages. They afford you time — time for strategy, innovation, and yes, even those margaritas (or a warm cup of tea, if that's your jam).

In essence, by adopting automation and embracing delegation, you're not only making space for business growth but personal growth. They're your allies in the quest for balance, ensuring you achieve entrepreneurial success without losing the essence of who you are.

Time Management Techniques: Mastering Your Minutes

Alright, lady bosses, time to put on our figurative capes and conquer time—or at least learn to use it efficiently. We've all heard it said that "time is money", but in the bustling world of business, time can also be sanity, relaxation, innovation, and that elusive work-life balance we're all after. Let's dive into strategies that can transform your hours from fleeting to fruitful.

Prioritize Like a Pro: The Eisenhower Box
This technique is all about discerning the urgent from the important. Picture a box, split into four:

1. Urgent and Important: These are your crises and pressing problems. Handle these immediately.
2. Not Urgent but Important: Strategy sessions, long-term planning. Schedule these in and protect the time.
3. Urgent but Not Important: Some emails, certain meetings. Can you delegate these?
4. Not Urgent and Not Important: Time wasters. Do these later, or perhaps even eliminate them.

The Magic of Time Blocking
Instead of to-do lists that stretch longer than a Monday morning, try time blocking. Allocate specific chunks of time to tasks and stick to them. It's like high school timetables, but you're the principal, teacher, and student rolled into one.

Pomodoro Technique: Short Bursts, Big Results
Named after a tomato-shaped timer (yep, really!), this technique advocates for working intensely for 25 minutes and then taking a 5-minute break. Repeat. It's surprisingly effective in maintaining focus and reducing the allure of distractions.

The Two-Minute Rule
Got a task that'll take less than two minutes? Do it now. This simple rule can clear small tasks that otherwise pile up.

Know Thyself: Peak Times and Energy Slumps
We all have our rhythm. Some of us are night owls, and others, early birds. Understand when you're at your peak in terms of energy and schedule your most demanding tasks for that time.

Embrace the Tech:
There's a slew of apps out there designed to help you with time management. From Trello for task management to RescueTime for tracking your digital habits, don't shy away from using technology to your advantage.

In the grand mosaic of entrepreneurship, each minute is a precious tile. And with these time management techniques, you're not just placing them haphazardly; you're crafting a masterpiece. Here's to less stress, more success, and the kind of efficiency that leaves room for a spontaneous mid-week movie night or that novel collecting dust on your shelf. Because, remember, managing time is also about making time for living.

Mindfulness and Meditation: Unlocking Clarity Amidst Chaos

Take a moment and think about the number of tabs open in your browser. Now think about the tabs open in your mind.

The outstanding invoice, the school recital, the client meeting tomorrow, the groceries. It's no wonder our mental browsers often crash! Enter mindfulness and meditation, the tech support for the modern entrepreneurial woman's brain. So, let's deep-dive into this realm of peace and mental clarity.

1. Understanding Mindfulness:
Mindfulness is about being present—truly present—in the moment. It's not about silencing your thoughts, but rather noticing them, without judgment. It's the gentle art of paying attention to the 'now'. When was the last time you really tasted your coffee, felt its warmth, and didn't just chug it down as fuel?

2. Why Mindfulness for Business Women?
When applied to business, mindfulness can lead to better decision-making, increased creativity, reduced stress, and improved relationships with colleagues and clients. It's like a software update for your brain—fixing glitches and improving performance.

3. Starting Simple: Breath Awareness
The simplest way to start is by paying attention to your breath. Notice the rise and fall of your chest, the sensation of air entering and leaving your nostrils. When your mind wanders (and it will), gently bring it back to your breath.

4. Body Scanning:
A step further from breath awareness, body scanning is about paying attention to different parts of your body. It's a mental massage, highlighting areas of tension you weren't aware of.

5. Guided Meditation:
For those who feel a bit lost in the silence, guided meditations,

often available on apps or online platforms, can be a great way to start. A narrator guides you through a story or visualization, assisting in channeling your focus.

6. Establishing a Routine:
Like any habit, consistency is key. Start with just five minutes a day. Gradually, as you start to relish this peaceful pocket of time, you'll find yourself naturally extending it.

7. Mindfulness in Daily Tasks:
You don't have to be seated in the lotus position to practice mindfulness. Washing dishes, walking to the mailbox, or waiting in line - any moment can be a mindful moment.

8. Benefits Beyond Calm:
While relaxation is often a pleasant side effect, the true power of mindfulness and meditation lies in its capacity to reshape our brains for resilience, emotional intelligence, and enhanced cognitive abilities - invaluable traits for any business leader.

As businesswomen, we wear numerous hats, juggling tasks with the dexterity of a seasoned performer. Mindfulness and meditation offer a quiet sanctuary, a place to reset and recharge. Imagine facing business challenges not as tumultuous storms but as breezes, knowing you have the inner tools to navigate through. Welcome to the era of mind-powered leadership.

Balancing the Scales

In the vibrant dance of life and business, every step, misstep, and twirl contributes to our unique rhythm. As modern women forging paths in a dynamic world, understanding the art of balance is paramount. It's not about creating a stark divide

divide between work and life but seamlessly blending the two, understanding that one fuels the other.

The essence of this chapter is not to find a mythical equilibrium where everything is in perfect harmony but to arm you with tools and insights to navigate the beautiful chaos with grace. It's about recognizing when to push, when to pause, and when to celebrate.

Our businesses, just like our personal lives, will have their ebbs and flows. There will be times of intense hustle followed by moments of quiet reflection. In understanding work-life balance, we're not just striving for success in business but curating a life rich in experiences, connections, and moments of true presence.

So, as you turn this page and continue your entrepreneurial journey, remember this: balance isn't a destination, it's a continuous act of tuning, adjusting, and embracing the dance. To the women who aspire, inspire, and perspire, here's to crafting a symphony where both business and life sing in harmony.

CHAPTER 15:
The Future of Women In Business

In the annals of history, change is often led by visionaries who dare to challenge the status quo. As we stand on the precipice of tomorrow, there's a potent force stirring the winds of change: Women in business. This chapter is a toast to every woman who has ever dared to dream, to the trailblazers who paved the way and the ones currently shaping the contours of the business world.

It's an exciting era. Across industries, women are not just filling up spaces but defining them, challenging traditional norms and rewriting the business playbook. From startups rooted in garages to boardrooms of global conglomerates, there's a resounding voice asserting itself, echoing aspirations, ambitions, and transformative ideas.

But what does the horizon hold for women in business? How will the coming decades shape and be shaped by them? As we delve deeper into this chapter, we'll navigate the predictions, the aspirations, and the tangible shifts laying the foundation for the next generation of female entrepreneurs. It's more than a chapter; it's a clarion call to every woman: the future beckons, and it looks incredibly promising.

The Horizon Ahead: A Glimpse into the Future of Female Entrepreneurship

As the sun sets on one era, it dawns upon another, bringing with it new challenges, opportunities, and innovations. And when we gaze into the future of female entrepreneurship, the horizon is illuminated with dazzling potential. Let's embark on a journey into the predictions and aspirations that will shape the landscape for the next wave of female trailblazers.

1. The Rise of Women in Tech and STEM: Historically, fields like technology and STEM (Science, Technology, Engineering, and Mathematics) have been male-dominated. But forecasts suggest a seismic shift. As educational barriers are dismantled and more initiatives encourage girls to delve into these areas, we can anticipate a surge of female-led tech startups and innovations.

2. Redefining Workplace Dynamics: The corporate ladder will undergo a transformation, becoming more of a lattice. Hierarchical structures will give way to collaborative ecosystems where leadership roles are defined by competence and vision rather than gender.

3. Sustainability at the Core: The next generation of female entrepreneurs will champion businesses that not only seek profit but also prioritize the planet and its people. Expect a rise in enterprises built on sustainable models, ethical practices, and green innovations.

4. The Global Sisterhood Network: Geographical boundaries will blur, giving way to a global network of female entrepreneurs supporting, investing in, and collaborating with each other. This collective strength will accelerate change and

amplify success stories across continents.

5. Holistic Business Approaches: The businesses of tomorrow will be driven by a holistic approach that intertwines profitability with mental well-being, work-life balance, and emotional intelligence. The emphasis will shift from 'doing it all' to 'doing it mindfully.'

6. Embracing the Digital Frontier: The digital realm will be the playground for the next-gen female entrepreneur. Whether it's leveraging AI, delving into the metaverse, or capitalizing on virtual reality, women will be at the helm of digital revolutions.

Aspirations for the Upcoming Era:

It's not just about what we predict but also what we aspire to. We hope for a world where business schools, accelerators, and incubators have equal representation. A world where women don't have to choose between personal aspirations and professional ambitions. A world where every girl, irrespective of her background, believes she can be a leader, an innovator, or an entrepreneur.

In essence, the future of female entrepreneurship isn't just about numbers or revenues; it's about crafting a narrative of empowerment, innovation, and relentless ambition. It's a narrative where every woman has a voice, and where that voice echoes with the power to change the world.

Empowering the Next Wave: The Art of Mentorship and Community Involvement

In the grand tapestry of entrepreneurial success, there's a thread that often goes unnoticed, yet is invaluable: the act of giving back. By mentoring the next generation and actively engaging with the community, we don't just cement our legacy; we also lay the foundation for countless other women to rise.

The Ripple Effect of Mentorship:

Mentorship is more than just providing advice over a cup of coffee. It's about forging connections, sharing experiences, and offering guidance tailored to individual needs. By mentoring, you set into motion a ripple effect: you empower one woman, who then empowers another, creating a chain of upliftment.

1. Initiate Constructive Conversations: Be the sounding board that your mentee needs. Create a safe space for them to discuss their aspirations, fears, and challenges.
2. Share Unfiltered Experiences: Your journey, with its highs and lows, can offer invaluable insights. Don't just share the triumphs; talk about the stumbling blocks and how you overcame them.
3. Help Navigate the Business Landscape: From deciphering business contracts to offering insights on market trends, your expertise can help your mentee sidestep pitfalls.
4. Provide Opportunities: Introduce your mentee to industry contacts, recommend them for projects, or simply be their champion in larger business circles.

Giving Back to the Community:

Empowerment doesn't stop at mentorship. Immersing oneself in community initiatives amplifies positive change on a broader scale.

1. Host Workshops and Webinars: Share your knowledge on entrepreneurship, leadership, or industry-specific topics to enlighten budding entrepreneurs.
2. Collaborate with Non-Profits: Partner with organizations that resonate with your values. Whether it's women's rights, education, or environmental initiatives, your support can make a tangible difference.
3. Sponsorship and Scholarships: Offer scholarships to aspiring female entrepreneurs, sponsor community events, or fund projects that align with your vision of empowerment.
4. Create Inclusive Workspaces: If you're in a position of influence, advocate for diverse and inclusive workplaces. Prioritize hiring practices that uplift women, especially from underrepresented communities.

The Road Ahead:

The journey of entrepreneurship is as much about climbing to the pinnacle of success as it is about lifting others along the way. By mentoring and actively engaging with the community, you plant seeds that grow into mighty trees, sheltering and inspiring generations to come. In the grand scheme of things, it's not just about the legacy we leave behind, but the futures we help shape.

Rising Stars: Young Women Shattering the Glass Ceiling

In an entrepreneurial world often dominated by seasoned veterans, a new wave of young women are emerging, making their mark and redefining success. Their stories, infused with passion, innovation, and tenacity, serve as a testament to the boundless potential of the next generation. Let's dive into the inspiring journeys of these trailblazing young women who are not just dreaming but are living their dreams.

1. Whitney Wolfe Herd: The founder and CEO of Bumble, a revolutionary dating app that empowers women to make the first move. Starting her career at Tinder, Whitney faced adversity and challenges but turned those experiences into motivation to launch a billion-dollar company that prioritizes women's safety and control.
2. Jamie Kern Lima: Co-founder of IT Cosmetics, Jamie transformed her struggles with skin issues into a groundbreaking cosmetics company. With resilience and authenticity, she pitched her products countless times until landing a transformative QVC deal, eventually selling her company to L'Oréal for $1.2 billion in 2016.
3. Melanie Perkins: As one of the youngest female CEOs to be running a billion-dollar startup, Melanie co-founded Canva. The journey began with a yearbook design business in her college dorm room and evolved into a user-friendly graphic design platform. Today, Canva is valued at over $6 billion.
4. Sabrina Gonzalez Pasterski: Not a traditional entrepreneur, Sabrina is a physicist often cited as the "next Einstein". By the age of 22, she was recognized for her pioneering work in the field of quantum gravity, catching the attention of many, including Stephen Hawking. Her intellectual prowess underscores the message that women are revolutionizing every field imaginable.
5. Iyinoluwa Aboyeji: Co-founder of Andela, a company that identifies and develops software developers, and Flutterwave, a payments API that makes it easier to do business across Africa. Both ventures have attracted attention from global investors and have profoundly impacted the African tech ecosystem.

Each of these women began their journey with a dream and faced various challenges along the way. Their stories serve as testament to what is possible when passion meets perseverance. Their tales inspire the next generation of female entrepreneurs to think big, act fearlessly, and break barriers.

Global Movements and Initiatives: Supporting Women in Business on a Global Scale

The march towards gender equality in the business world is gaining momentum, not just on a community or national level but on a grand global scale. Several movements and initiatives worldwide have been dedicated to supporting, empowering, and celebrating women entrepreneurs, providing them with the tools, resources, and environments they need to succeed.

- WEConnect International: A global network that connects women-owned businesses to qualified buyers around the world. It identifies, educates, registers, and certifies women's business enterprises based outside of the U.S. that are at least 51% owned, managed, and controlled by one or more women.
- Women's Entrepreneurship Day (WED): Celebrated annually, WED works globally to empower women and girls to become active participants in the economy by igniting a network of women leaders, innovators, and entrepreneurs to initiate startups, drive economic expansion, and advance communities worldwide.
- Goldman Sachs 10,000 Women: This initiative offers women entrepreneurs around the world an integrated program of quality education, mentoring, and networking. It's built on the premise that providing women with a business and management education will lead to increased employment and more prosperous communities.
- SheTrades: A unique initiative of the International Trade Centre, a joint agency of the United Nations and the World Trade Organization, SheTrades seeks to connect three

million women entrepreneurs to the global market by 2021. They provide a digital platform, events, workshops, and more to achieve this ambitious goal.
- The Cherie Blair Foundation for Women: Cherie Blair, wife of former UK Prime Minister Tony Blair, established this foundation to help women build small and growing businesses in low and middle-income countries so they can contribute to their economies and have a stronger voice in their societies.
- Tory Burch Foundation: Established by fashion entrepreneur Tory Burch, this foundation offers capital, education, and resources to women, advocating for the empowerment of women entrepreneurs.

It's heartening to witness a global push towards uplifting women in business. With the support of such robust initiatives and movements, female entrepreneurs have more than just a fighting chance in the often challenging world of business—they have a thriving ecosystem that champions their potential, talent, and indomitable spirit.

While the journey towards full gender equality in business is ongoing, these initiatives exemplify a world coming together to uplift its women, showcasing a promising horizon for every aspiring female entrepreneur.

Legacy and Succession: Ensuring Your Business Thrives Beyond You

The journey of entrepreneurship, from inception to realization, is both intensely personal and, paradoxically, larger than oneself. Building a business is akin to birthing a legacy, one that many hope will outlive them and continue to influence and inspire.

The idea of legacy is about looking ahead, making a mark, and establishing a foundation for future generations. For the passionate businesswoman, ensuring that her venture thrives beyond her era involves careful planning, foresight, and a deep understanding of succession. Here's a breakdown of the significance of legacy and the mechanics of ensuring a successful transition.

- Understanding the Weight of Legacy: At the heart of every businesswoman's journey is a narrative—a story of trials, tribulations, victories, and learnings. This story, rich with experience and insight, is a part of the legacy that's passed on. It's a beacon for future leaders, giving them direction and clarity.
- Identifying Potential Successors: A crucial step in ensuring your business continues to prosper is identifying and grooming potential successors. Whether it's a family member, a trusted employee, or an external recruit, the individual should resonate with the brand's ethos and have the vision to carry forward its legacy.
- Knowledge Transfer: A smooth transition demands an extensive transfer of knowledge. This includes understanding the intricacies of the business, its history, key relationships, and operational nuances. Structured mentorship programs can facilitate this.
- Legal Aspects of Succession: Beyond the personal and operational facets of succession lies the legal dimension. Drafting a clear will, setting up trusts, or creating buy-sell agreements can ensure that the transfer of leadership and ownership is seamless and free from disputes.
- Emotional Transition: Stepping back from a business you've nurtured can be emotionally challenging. It's essential to acknowledge these feelings and seek support, whether through mentorship, counseling, or peer networks.

- Advisory Roles and Continued Guidance: Many businesswomen choose to stay connected with their ventures post-succession in advisory capacities. This allows them to provide guidance without directly controlling day-to-day operations.
- Reinvention and New Beginnings: Succession doesn't spell the end for the entrepreneur. Many see it as an opportunity for reinvention—a chance to explore new ventures, offer mentorship, or even indulge in pursuits outside the business realm.

The importance of creating a lasting legacy is paramount. For the modern woman entrepreneur, it's about crafting a narrative of endurance, empowerment, and evolution—a narrative that not only chronicles her journey but also paves the way for those who follow. Through careful succession planning, this narrative continues, echoing the values, visions, and vigor of its originator, ensuring that the business not only survives but thrives and flourishes in the times to come.

Love Languages of Business

The concept of love languages was famously introduced by Dr. Gary Chapman in his bestselling book, "The Five Love Languages." While his insights were initially meant to enhance personal relationships, it's uncanny how applicable they are to the realm of business, especially when considering customer relations. As a savvy female entrepreneur, understanding these "business love languages" can be a game-changer in cultivating loyalty, trust, and meaningful connections with your customers. Let's translate these languages into actionable strategies for your enterprise:

1. Words of Affirmation

Personal Translation: You thrive on feedback and positive affirmation.
Business Application: Engage in active communication with your clients. Send thank-you emails, post appreciative messages, or spotlight loyal customers on your social media platforms. Your customers will feel seen and valued, encouraging brand loyalty.

2. Acts of Service

Personal Translation: You show love through actions and meaningful contributions.
Business Application: Offer after-sales service, free workshops, webinars, or additional support. It shows your dedication and commitment to ensuring customer satisfaction beyond the purchase.

3. Receiving Gifts

Personal Translation: You feel loved when given thoughtful gifts.
Business Application: Incorporate occasional giveaways, loyalty rewards, or exclusive deals. The thought behind these tokens can resonate deeply with customers, making them feel cherished and valued.

4. Quality Time

Personal Translation: For you, spending undivided time is the purest expression of love.

Business Application: Host Q&A sessions, live product demos, or virtual coffee chats. Offering undivided attention fosters deeper customer relationships, emphasizing their significance to your brand.

5. Physical Touch

Personal Translation: In personal life, this may mean hugs or touch. In business, it translates differently.
Business Application: Think tactile experiences: the unboxing experience of a product, the ambiance in your physical store, or even the user experience on your website. Make these interactions as smooth and pleasurable as possible.

Leveraging Your Giving Love Language:

Every entrepreneur has her dominant love language when it comes to engaging with customers. Embrace it. If Words of Affirmation is your strength, focus on content creation, newsletters, and personalized messages. If Acts of Service resonate more, emphasize stellar customer service and post-sale engagements.

By understanding and implementing these love languages in business, you'll not only forge deeper connections with your customers but will also harness your natural inclinations to offer unparalleled value. In the world of business, where genuine connection can sometimes be overlooked, employing the love languages can set you apart and pave the way for sustainable, heartfelt success.

Women and the Future Tapestry of Business
The trajectory of women in business is not just a line, it's a spectrum —a rainbow of possibilities, innovation, and

trailblazing leadership. As we've journeyed through this chapter, we've encountered the luminous tales of young entrepreneurs, the empowering wave of global movements, and even the intricate dance of translating love languages into business acumen.

The path ahead for women in business is vast, stretching beyond horizons we can currently see. Each day, more glass ceilings are shattered, more traditional norms are questioned, and new avenues are explored. It's not just about thriving in the present but setting a foundation for future generations of ambitious women, ensuring that the entrepreneurial world they step into is even more inclusive, diverse, and primed for success.

However, while the future is filled with promise, it also requires intention. As female entrepreneurs, our responsibility is not just to our businesses but to the community of women in the industry. By mentoring, by sharing, by championing each other, we aren't just building individual enterprises but an entire empire of women-led innovation.

Here's to the future—a future where women aren't just participants in the business world but significant drivers of its evolution. Through collaboration, resilience, and a never-ending zeal for learning, we are scripting a narrative that will inspire generations to come. So, as we close this chapter, remember: The future isn't just something that happens; it's something we create. And women, with their tenacity, vision, and passion, are at the forefront of crafting a business landscape that's not just profitable but profoundly impactful.

CONCLUSION

As we reach the culmination of this transformative journey, it's imperative to pause, reflect, and recognize the brilliance within you. Through each chapter, from mastering the nuances of AI to the delicate balance of work-life, from the future possibilities for women in business to the art of storytelling and branding, the key takeaway is clear: the world of business is vast, but your unique space within it is irreplaceable.

It's often said that the best time to plant a tree was twenty years ago, and the second best time is now. Similarly, irrespective of where you are in your entrepreneurial journey, this moment—right now—is teeming with possibility. It's your opportunity to mold, reshape, and reinvent. The canvas of the business world is vast, and you hold the brush.

Remember, the path to success isn't linear. There will be peaks of exhilaration and valleys of doubt. There will be days when the weight of challenges might seem overwhelming, but then there will be moments where the thrill of a breakthrough will make it all worthwhile. Embrace it all, for every experience is a stepping stone, carving your unique path.

Equipped with the knowledge, insights, and tools from this

book, you're no longer merely a participant in the entrepreneurial world; you're a game-changer. Your vision, your passion, and your perseverance are the trinity that will drive your success. And while the journey might sometimes feel solitary, know that you're part of a burgeoning community of women who are not just dreaming but doing, not just planning but executing.

The world of business, as expansive as it is, awaits your touch, your flair, and your unique brand of magic. So, dear reader, as you close this book and embark on your own journey, always remember: you are not just destined for greatness; you are the very embodiment of it. Your time isn't coming; it's already here. Illuminate the business realm with your brilliance, for now, more than ever, it's your time to shine.

As we stand at the precipice of a new era in business, there's an unmistakable call to action that resounds in the corridors of enterprises, boardrooms, and startups alike. That call? To challenge and change the long-standing status quo.

For far too long, the business landscape has been shaped by paradigms and principles that, while historically significant, don't necessarily serve the diverse and dynamic world we live in today. Especially for women, the time has come to usher in change. No longer are we content to simply fit into the mold created by others. Instead, we are carving out spaces, redefining standards, and leading revolutions in thought and action.

The challenge lies not just in recognizing the areas that need evolution, but in actively spearheading that transformation. It's about asking the hard questions: Why is this the way it is? Can it be better? More inclusive? More innovative? How can I, as a woman in business, lead this change?

While these questions are the start, action is the fulcrum. To change the status quo is to be unafraid of being the first, of being the voice that rises above the murmur, of being the hand that crafts a new direction. It's about leveraging the collective power of women, pooling our resources, knowledge, and passions to break barriers and set new standards.

The world of business, as we know it, is on the cusp of a renaissance. A renaissance led by women who are no longer waiting for permission but are granting it to themselves. Women who understand that to change the game; sometimes, you have to change the rules.

So, to every woman reading this, the call is clear and resonant: The business world is your realm, and within it lies the power and potential to challenge and alter the age-old status quo. Rise, lead, innovate, and pave the way for a future where the business narrative is as diverse, dynamic, and inclusive as the world it serves.

100 Days of Mantras

Day 1: "I am the architect of my success."
Day 2: "Limitations live only in our minds; possibilities are endless."
Day 3: "Every setback is a setup for a comeback."
Day 4: "Ambition is my compass, resilience is my north star."
Day 5: "Empowered women empower women."
Day 6: "I turn challenges into opportunities."
Day 7: "I am fierce, I am focused, I am fearless."
Day 8: "Success isn't given; it's earned with passion and perseverance."
Day 9: "Failure is just feedback, and feedback is the breakfast of champions."
Day 10: "Doubt kills more dreams than failure ever will."
Day 11: "In the orchestra of success, I choose to lead, not follow."
Day 12: "My dreams are valid, my hustle is real."
Day 13: "Success is the intersection of preparation and opportunity."
Day 14: "I thrive because I believe in my journey and trust my process."
Day 15: "Every 'No' leads me closer to a 'Yes'."
Day 16: "I rise by lifting others."
Day 17: "In the story of success, grit is the unsung hero."
Day 18: "Today's risks are tomorrow's stories of triumph."
Day 19: "The best way to predict the future is to create it."
Day 20: "Success is sweetest when shared."
Day 21: "I grow, I evolve, I conquer."
Day 22: "My ambition isn't a ceiling; it's the sky."
Day 23: "When they go low, I go high."
Day 24: "I believe in the magic that happens outside the

comfort zone."
Day 25: "I am my best investment."
Day 26: "The hustle is real, but so are the rewards."
Day 27: "Where there's passion, there's purpose."
Day 28: "Champion mindset, every single day."
Day 29: "My journey, my pace, my success story."
Day 30: "Daring greatly, leading boldly."
Day 31: "The power within me is greater than any obstacle before me."
Day 32: "Growth and comfort do not coexist."
Day 33: "Visionaries see the impossible as the inevitable."
Day 34: "Every challenge met is a step closer to my dream."
Day 35: "I am my biggest project and greatest success."
Day 36: "Dream it. Believe it. Achieve it."
Day 37: "Empowerment starts within."
Day 38: "Every venture teaches me something new."
Day 39: "Driven by passion, guided by purpose."
Day 40: "Bold actions define bold leaders."
Day 41: "I bloom from every place I've ever been buried."
Day 42: "Change is the only constant in business and life."
Day 43: "Opportunities don't wait. Neither do I."
Day 44: "Innovate, elevate, and dominate."
Day 45: "I'm the CEO of my destiny."
Day 46: "Business is about creating impact, not just income."
Day 47: "Every risk taken is a step forward."
Day 48: "I cultivate success from my failures."
Day 49: "The world needs what I have to offer."
Day 50: "Fueling my dreams with ambition and action."
Day 51: "My potential is limitless."
Day 52: "Courage over comfort every time."
Day 53: "Building bridges, not walls."
Day 54: "I radiate success and attract prosperity."
Day 55: "My success is shaped by perseverance, not perfection."

Day 56: "Leading with grace, succeeding with grit."
Day 57: "Every no gets me closer to my next yes."
Day 58: "I embrace challenges as growth opportunities."
Day 59: "Where others see obstacles, I see opportunities."
Day 60: "Victory favors the tenacious."
Day 61: "Rising up with resilience and resolve."
Day 62: "Chasing dreams, not competition."
Day 63: "Every day is a new chapter in my success story."
Day 64: "Making choices today that my future self will thank me for."
Day 65: "I am built from every mistake I've ever made."
Day 66: "The universe has my back."
Day 67: "With every failure, I grow stronger and smarter."
Day 68: "I'm the author of my narrative."
Day 69: "Manifesting abundance with every move."
Day 70: "I am the change I wish to see."
Day 71: "Breaking barriers with brilliance and bravery."
Day 72: "I don't wait for luck; I create it."
Day 73: "Shattering ceilings, one goal at a time."
Day 74: "Embracing every part of my journey."
Day 75: "I wear challenges as badges of honor."
Day 76: "Bringing my dreams to life with unwavering focus."
Day 77: "The harder I work, the luckier I get."
Day 78: "I am more than capable of manifesting my aspirations."
Day 79: "With persistence, every goal is attainable."
Day 80: "Destiny favors the driven."
Day 81: "Crafting a legacy of leadership."
Day 82: "I am the master of my fate."
Day 83: "Success is my only option."
Day 84: "Creating ripples of positive change."
Day 85: "Pushing boundaries, setting new standards."

Day 86: "Every brick they threw, I used to build my empire."
Day 87: "I'm powered by purpose and coffee."
Day 88: "Transforming vision into victory."
Day 89: "Where there's a will, I'm the way."
Day 90: "Blazing my trail, setting my pace."
Day 91: "Building dreams, one goal at a time."
Day 92: "I believe in the power of yet."
Day 93: "Success doesn't come to you; you go to it."
Day 94: "Every mountain climbed starts with a step."
Day 95: "Defining my destiny with determination."
Day 96: "Limitless in potential, limitless in impact."
Day 97: "Being fearless in the pursuit of what sets my soul on fire."
Day 98: "Success is the sum of small efforts repeated."
Day 99: "Passionate about progress, not perfection."
Day 100: "With every obstacle, I become more unstoppable."

100 Business Ideas

- Eco-Fashion Designer: Designing sustainable clothing lines using eco-friendly materials.
- Herbalist: Crafting and selling herbal remedies or organic teas.
- Virtual Fitness Trainer: Offering online classes or personal training sessions.
- Art Therapist: Helping individuals express themselves and heal through art.
- Ethical Beauty Product Creator: Formulating organic, cruelty-free cosmetics.
- Tech-Wellness Consultant: Helping people find tech solutions to enhance well-being.
- Podcast Producer: Focusing on niche topics ranging from motherhood to tech news.
- Childproofing Expert: Helping parents make their homes safe for babies and toddlers.
- Mobile Spa Owner: Providing spa services at client's homes or corporate offices.
- Personal Chef for Special Diets: Catering to vegan, gluten-free, or other dietary needs.
- Space Organizer: Offering home or office decluttering and organizing services.
- Local Tour Guide: Organizing unique experiences in one's city or town.
- e-Book Publisher: Writing or helping others publish digital books.
- Custom Jewelry Maker: Crafting unique jewelry pieces, possibly from upcycled materials.
- Online Education Consultant: Setting up e-learning platforms for schools or corporations.

- Homemade Gourmet Food Producer: Making jams, sauces, or baked goods for sale.
- Subscription Box Curator: Monthly boxes with niche products (e.g., eco-friendly household items).
- Agricultural Innovator: Urban farming or creating vertical gardens.
- Mobile Veterinarian: Providing pet health services at the pet owner's location.
- Elderly Activity Planner: Organizing events and activities for seniors.
- Niche Subscription Magazine Editor: For topics like local arts, kids' activities, or health.
- Digital Art Merchant: Selling digital art prints or designs online.
- Fair-Trade Goods Retailer: Selling ethically sourced products.
- Holistic Nutritionist: Offering diet and lifestyle consulting based on holistic principles.
- Pet Care Products Developer: Organic pet foods, toys, or accessories.
- Home Decorator for Renters: Specializing in non-permanent, stylish home solutions.
- DIY Craft Kit Seller: Assembling materials and instructions for craft projects.
- Sustainable Event Planner: Planning eco-friendly events or weddings.
- Dance Instructor: Teaching unique dance forms, perhaps for couples or pregnant women.
- Travel Planner for Moms: Organizing family-friendly or moms-only getaways.
- Freelance Researcher: Helping businesses gather data and insights.
- Homemade Skincare Producer: Creating organic lotions, creams, or soaps.

- Children's App Developer: Making educational or entertainment apps for kids.
- Online Art Teacher: Offering lessons in painting, sculpture, or other forms.
- Home Bakery Owner: Selling cakes, pastries, or bread from home.
- Financial Coach for Women: Assisting women in managing and investing their finances.
- Eco-Tourism Operator: Running green travel experiences in natural settings.
- Sustainable Toy Maker: Crafting toys from organic or recycled materials.
- Boutique Bed & Breakfast Owner: Running a unique, themed B&B.
- Handmade Candle Maker: Using eco-friendly wax and natural scents.
- Recycled Furniture Designer: Upcycling old furniture into stylish pieces.
- Tailored Children's Book Author: Personalizing stories for individual children.
- Local Art Dealer: Representing local artists and selling their works.
- Nutrition Blogger: Offering tips, recipes, and product reviews.
- Online Yoga Instructor: Conducting yoga classes through streaming platforms.
- Freelance Graphic Designer: Specializing in branding for female entrepreneurs.
- Eco-Conscious Packaging Consultant: Helping businesses reduce waste in their packaging.
- Themed Experience Planner: Organizing themed parties or date nights.
- Mindfulness Retreat Organizer: Hosting wellness and meditation retreats.

- Pop-up Shop Organizer: Setting up temporary retail spaces for various products.
- Home Renovation Consultant: Focusing on sustainable, green renovations.
- Personal Shopping Assistant: For fashion, groceries, or gifts.
- Health-Focused Cooking Instructor: Offering classes on vegan, paleo, or other diets.
- Mobile Art Gallery Owner: Showcasing art in different locations.
- Ethical Coffee Supplier: Sourcing and selling fair-trade coffee.
- Digital Marketing Specialist: Assisting businesses with their online presence.
- Homemade Crafts Retailer: Selling crafts through online platforms.
- Voice-Over Artist: For advertisements, animation, or e-learning.
- Workshop Facilitator: On topics ranging from business skills to personal growth.
- Ethical Clothing Retailer: Selling eco-friendly and ethically-made apparel.
- Freelance Writer or Editor: Writing for websites, magazines, or corporate clients.
- Board Game Developer: Creating unique and engaging board games.
- Children's Activity Book Author: Focusing on educational or creative tasks.
- Culinary Tour Operator: Organizing food tours in local cities.
- Personalized Jewelry Maker: Crafting jewelry based on client preferences.
- Childcare Service Provider: Offering specialized care, like bilingual babysitting.

- Eco-friendly Cleaning Service: Using green products for home cleaning.
- Brand Consultant: Helping businesses craft and refine their brand image.
- Community Workshop Space Owner: Renting out space for local events and workshops.
- Online Course Creator: Offering courses on platforms like Udemy or Coursera.
- Custom Footwear Designer: Crafting unique shoes based on client specifications.
- Tech Consultant for Seniors: Assisting the elderly with modern technology.
- Gardening Expert: Helping people set up and maintain their gardens.
- Freelance Photographer: Specializing in events, products, or portraits.
- Sustainable Travel Blogger: Sharing eco-friendly travel tips and locations.
- Virtual Reality Experience Creator: Designing VR experiences for education or entertainment.
- Home Stylist: Assisting clients in decorating their homes.
- Mental Health Blogger: Sharing personal stories and advice.
- Freelance Translator: Offering translation services in one or more languages.
- Handcrafted Pottery Seller: Creating and selling unique pottery items.
- Themed Cafe Owner: Such as book cafes, cat cafes, or board game cafes.
- Freelance Social Media Manager: Managing online profiles for businesses.
- Custom Perfume Creator: Crafting scents based on individual preferences.
- Eco-friendly Wedding Planner: Organizing green and sustainable weddings.

- Digital Nomad Blogger: Sharing tips and experiences about working remotely.
- Handmade Stationery Designer: Creating journals, greeting cards, and more.
- Natural Dye Producer: For fabrics and crafts.
- Language Tutor: Teaching languages online or in person.
- Online Boutique Owner: Selling curated or handmade items.
- Female Empowerment Coach: Offering courses and coaching for women's personal growth.
- Custom Toy Maker: Crafting toys based on children's drawings or ideas.
- Elderly Companion Service: Providing companionship and assistance to the elderly.
- Vegan Bakery Owner: Selling vegan pastries and sweets.
- Personal Branding Consultant: Assisting individuals in building their personal brand.
- Natural Cosmetics Workshop Host: Teaching people to make their cosmetics.
- Mystery Event Planner: Organizing surprise events for birthdays or anniversaries.
- Upcycled Clothing Designer: Transforming old clothes into new designs.
- Ethical Chocolate Producer: Making and selling fair-trade chocolates.
- Handmade Soap Workshop Facilitator: Teaching the craft of soap-making.
- Community Network Builder: Creating platforms or events for local networking.

Business Checklist

1. Self-Assessment:
- [] Determine why you want to start a business.
- [] Evaluate your skills, strengths, and weaknesses.
- [] Assess your risk tolerance.

2. Market Research:
- [] Identify a business idea or industry based on your interests.
- [] Conduct market research to validate demand.
- [] Identify target customers.
- [] Analyze your competitors.

3. Business Planning:
- [] Define your business's mission and vision.
- [] Outline your business goals (short-term and long-term).
- [] Draft a business plan detailing your strategy, operations, and financial projections.

4. Legal Requirements:
- [] Decide on a business structure (sole proprietorship, LLC, corporation, etc.).
- [] Register your business name.
- [] Obtain the necessary licenses and permits.
- [] Get an Employer Identification Number (EIN) for tax purposes.
- [] Ensure you're compliant with local, state, and federal regulations.
- [] Draft partnership or shareholder agreements if applicable.

5. Finances:
- [] Open a business bank account.
- [] Determine your startup costs.
- [] Develop a pricing strategy.
- [] Create a budget.
- [] Plan your funding strategy (e.g., personal savings, bank loans, angel investors, crowdfunding).

6. Branding and Marketing:
- [] Design a business logo and tagline.
- [] Secure a domain name and set up a professional email.
- [] Develop a company website.
- [] Create business profiles on social media platforms.
- [] Develop a marketing and advertising strategy.

7. Operations:
- [] Find a business location (if needed).
- [] Plan the supply chain and inventory management (for product-based businesses).
- [] Set up an accounting system.
- [] Consider business insurance needs.
- [] Hire employees if necessary. Ensure compliance with labor laws.

8. Networking and Growth:
- [] Join local business chambers or industry-specific associations.
- [] Attend networking events and trade shows.
- [] Seek mentorship or advice from established entrepreneurs.
- [] Consider collaborating with complementary businesses.

9. Technology and Tools:
- [] Choose the necessary software tools (accounting, CRM, marketing automation).
- [] Ensure your business has the necessary tech infrastructure (hardware, connectivity).
- [] Develop a cybersecurity plan.

10. Launch Preparation:
- [] Develop a launch strategy.
- [] Gather feedback through beta testing or pilot programs.
- [] Plan a launch event or promotion.

11. Continuous Learning:
- [] Stay updated with industry news and trends.
- [] Consider further education or courses to enhance business skills.
- [] Regularly review and adapt your business plan based on feedback and performance.

Monthly Business Challenge

JANUARY CHALLENGE:

The start of a new year holds the promise of fresh opportunities, new ventures, and the chance to reinvent or improve upon what we've built. As the saying goes, "If you fail to plan, you are planning to fail." January is the time to not only set goals but to map out the intricate pathways that will lead to your targets.

Week 1: Self-reflection and Assessment
- Task: Before you charge ahead, take a step back. Reflect on the previous year. What worked? What didn't? Which strategies paid off, and which ones need rethinking?
- Activity: Dedicate a day for reflection. Journal your thoughts, insights, and learnings from the past year. Consider it a debrief to yourself.

Week 2: Define Clear Objectives
- Task: Once you've assessed the lay of the land, pinpoint your primary business goal for the year. It should be specific, measurable, achievable, relevant, and time-bound (SMART).
- Activity: Draft your goal statement and place it where you can see it daily. This constant visibility serves as a daily nudge, reminding you of your purpose.

Week 3: Actionable Steps
- Task: A goal without a plan can quickly become a distant dream. Break your primary goal into sub-goals or milestones. From there, detail the specific actions needed to achieve each one.

- Activity: Create a visual representation of your goal's roadmap. This could be a flowchart, a timeline, or any format that resonates with you. The idea is to make your path clear, compelling, and actionable.

Week 4: Accountability System
- Task: Establishing goals is essential, but ensuring you're on track is equally vital. Set up a monthly or bi-monthly check-in system where you assess your progress.
- Activity: Schedule these check-ins on your calendar for the entire year. Consider involving a business mentor, coach, or trusted colleague to hold you accountable.

Bonus Activity: Vision Board Party
A vision board is a collage of images, pictures, and affirmations that represent your dreams and goals. Hosting a vision board party can be an exciting way to bring together like-minded entrepreneurs to share aspirations and dreams. Here's how to make the most of it:

1. Preparation: Send out invites (virtual or physical) and ask participants to think about their goals in advance.
2. Materials: Ensure you have ample magazines, scissors, glue, markers, and large poster boards. For virtual sessions, apps like Canva or Pinterest can be utilized.
3. Guidance: Start the session with a brief talk on the importance of visualizing goals. You could invite a guest speaker or provide this guidance yourself.
4. Sharing: Once everyone has created their boards, allow time for sharing. This step can be motivating as it creates a sense of community and shared ambition.

End January on a high, with clarity in vision, a roadmap in hand, and the motivation of shared dreams.

February Challenge

Ah, finances. They're the unsung hero behind any thriving business. As the month of love, February asks us to cherish and respect our financial relationships just as much as our personal ones. So, let's make financial decisions that our future selves will thank us for.

Week 1: Understanding Last Year's Financials
- Day 1-3: Dive deep into your previous year's balance sheet, income statement, and cash flow statement.
- Day 4-5: Identify the revenue streams that were most successful and the expenses that can be reconsidered.
- Day 6-7: Host a discussion (or reflection, if you're solo) about unexpected financial challenges faced last year and brainstorm ways to tackle them if they recur.

Week 2: Setting Financial Milestones
- Day 8: Define a clear financial goal for February.
- Day 9-10: Segment this monthly goal into weekly targets to make it more achievable.
- Day 11-13: Develop a tracking system to monitor daily expenses and revenues.
- Day 14: Treat yourself to something small (but delightful!) for maintaining a week of financial discipline.

Week 3: Embracing Financial Mindfulness
- Day 15-17: Explore financial tools or apps that can assist in daily financial tracking.
- Day 18-19: Dedicate some time to read a financial article or book that can offer new insights or strategies.
- Day 20-21: Evaluate your financial commitments: subscriptions, memberships, and recurring expenses. Are there any you can do without or find alternatives for?

Week 4: Financial Growth and Security
- Day 22-23: Explore potential areas in your business that promise a solid ROI and consider allocating a budget towards them.
- Day 24-25: Delve into your business insurance and future investments. Are you adequately covered? Are there better investment opportunities?
- Day 26-28: Create a "rainy day" fund, if you haven't already, and commit to contributing to it regularly.

Bonus Activities:
- Networking with Finance Gurus: Set up coffee dates or virtual meet-ups with finance-savvy folks in your circle or industry. Their experiences and advice can be priceless.
- Financial Workshops: Dive into a short online workshop or seminar on a specific financial topic of interest.

At the end of the month, reward yourself for the dedication to financial health. Perhaps it's time for that book you've been eyeing, or a nice evening out (or in, with a special treat). Remember, financial discipline doesn't mean denying yourself pleasures but enjoying them responsibly.

March Challenge

March heralds the anticipation of spring, a time of renewal and growth. Similarly, this month is dedicated to rejuvenating your marketing strategies, breathing life into how you present your business to the world. Let's step out of our comfort zones, experiment with fresh tactics, and cultivate our brand's blooming presence.

Week 1: Understanding Your Audience
- Day 1-2: Deep dive into your customer analytics. Who are they? What do they resonate with?
- Day 3-4: Develop user personas if you haven't already. This helps in tailoring your marketing messages.
- Day 5-6: Run a quick survey or feedback session with some of your customers to understand their changing needs or preferences.
- Day 7: Reflect on this newfound knowledge. How can your product or service evolve to cater to these insights?

Week 2: Experimenting with New Platforms and Content
- Day 8-9: Choose a new social media platform or marketing channel you haven't leveraged. Understand its mechanics.
- Day 10-12: Draft a content plan for this platform. Could be daily posts, stories, or even ads.
- Day 13-14: Execute. Put out the content and monitor engagement levels.

Week 3: Ad Strategy and Campaign Building
- Day 15-16: Research and understand the nuances of a new ad strategy. Could be PPC, native advertising, influencer marketing, or anything else you're unfamiliar with.
- Day 17-19: Outline the campaign, set a budget, and define the target audience.

- Day 20-21: Launch the campaign. Monitor the initial response.

Week 4: Analyze, Optimize, Repeat
- Day 22-23: Analyze the outcomes of your new marketing efforts. What worked? What didn't?
- Day 24-25: Engage with your audience. Reply to comments, thank people for sharing, and engage in discussions.
- Day 26-28: Optimize based on insights. Tweak the strategy to better cater to your audience.

Day 29-31 (if applicable): Reflect on the entire month's efforts. What lessons have been learned? What can be carried forward into the next month?

Bonus Activities:
- Collaborative Campaign: Collaborate with another entrepreneur or brand. This could be a joint webinar, a shared product discount, or co-created content.
- Marketing Workshop: Take an online course or workshop on a particular marketing topic. Continuous learning keeps us ahead in this dynamic field.

By month-end, you'd have not only tried a new marketing strategy but gauged its effectiveness, ready to springboard into the rest of the year with a refreshed and more informed approach. Cheers to a March filled with masterful marketing moves!

April Challenge

April is a month of blossoming flowers and warmer days, making it the perfect backdrop for growing connections and expanding horizons. As an entrepreneur, networking is the lifeline that fuels opportunities, ideas, and collaborations. This month, challenge yourself to not just attend events but to truly engage and amplify your business's reach.

Week 1: Research and Registration
- Day 1-2: Begin by identifying online and local networking events, webinars, or workshops related to your industry or field of interest.
- Day 3-4: Register for the ones that resonate with your goals and schedule them in your calendar.
- Day 5-6: Prepare for these events: Update your business cards, work on your elevator pitch, and list down talking points or questions.
- Day 7: Reflect on your networking goals. What do you want to achieve from these events?

Week 2: First Event Attendance
- Day 8-9: Attend your first event or webinar. Take notes and actively participate.
- Day 10-11: Follow up with new contacts you've made. A personalized email or message can set the foundation for a strong professional relationship.
- Day 12-13: Review your experience. What went well? What can you improve for the next event?
- Day 14: Rest, recharge, and mentally prepare for the next event.

Week 3: Second Event & Collaboration Ideas
- Day 15-16: Attend your second event or webinar. Engage, ask questions, and be sure to introduce yourself to new faces.
- Day 17-18: Again, follow up with any new contacts. Consider setting up one-on-one virtual coffee chats with those who align with your business vision.
- Day 19-20: Brainstorm potential collaboration ideas. With whom can you see a partnership flourishing?
- Day 21: Reach out to potential collaborators. Propose a joint venture or promotion.

Week 4: Deepen Connections
- Day 22-23: Dedicate time to nurturing your new connections. This can mean sharing their content, referring clients, or offering feedback.
- Day 24-25: Host or attend a more intimate networking event, like a round-table discussion or panel in your industry.
- Day 26-28: Reflect on the month's networking efforts. How have these connections added value to your business?
- Day 29-30 (if applicable): Draft a plan for maintaining these connections in the coming months. Remember, networking is a continuous effort.

Bonus Activities:
- Joint Venture: Host a joint webinar, workshop, or event with a fellow entrepreneur or business. Sharing platforms can introduce you to their audience and vice versa.
- Social Shoutouts: Spotlight a business you connected with this month on your social channels. It's all about mutual growth.

April's endeavours will lay down the foundation for exciting collaborations, knowledge exchange, and opportunities in the months ahead.

May Challenge

May, the month where flowers bloom in abundance, reminds us of growth and gratitude. As we appreciate nature's beauty, let's also turn our attention to those who have helped our businesses bloom: our customers. This month, let's deepen our connection with our customers by showing them just how much we value their trust and loyalty.

Week 1: Preparation and Planning
- Day 1-2: Take a deep dive into your customer data. Understand their preferences, buying patterns, and feedback.
- Day 3-4: Design your 'Thank You' campaign. Decide if you want to offer discounts, exclusive content, or perhaps a freebie.
- Day 5-6: Draft personalized thank you notes or messages for your top customers. Authenticity goes a long way.
- Day 7: Choose a platform to spotlight a loyal customer. This could be your website's homepage, a social media post, or your newsletter.

Week 2: The Rollout
- Day 8-9: Officially launch your 'Thank You' campaign. Spread the word across all your platforms.
- Day 10-11: Share the spotlighted customer story. Talk about their journey with your business.
- Day 12-13: Engage with customers actively. Respond to their queries, comments, or any feedback they might provide.
- Day 14: Reflect on the campaign's first week. Are customers responding positively? Do you need to tweak anything?

Week 3: Amplifying Appreciation
- Day 15-16: Send out a newsletter highlighting testimonials or stories from satisfied customers.

- Day 17-18: Host a live Q&A session or a webinar for customers, addressing any of their concerns and showcasing upcoming products or services.
- Day 19-20: Share behind-the-scenes content, offering customers an inside look into your business processes.
- Day 21: Ask customers for feedback and reviews. This not only offers valuable insights but shows you value their opinions.

Week 4: Culmination and Continuation
- Day 22-23: Offer a special deal or flash sale for your most loyal customers. A surprise discount can solidify their loyalty further.
- Day 24-25: Share user-generated content. Repost photos or testimonials customers have shared about your product/service.
- Day 26-28: Reflect on the entire campaign. What worked best? What could be improved?
 Day 29-30: Start planning ways to integrate customer appreciation as a regular part of your business strategy.

Bonus Activities:
- Feedback Forum: Create an interactive space (online forum, social media poll) where customers can provide suggestions or ideas for your business.
- Showcase Testimonials: Dedicate a section of your website or social media to showcase customer testimonials or reviews, allowing prospects to see the value you provide.

May's endeavors will not only nurture the bond with your current customers but also instill trust in potential ones. A business that values and appreciates its customers stands out in the vast entrepreneurial landscape.

June Challenge

June, with its long days and bright sunlight, beckons a fresh wave of energy and optimism. As we transition to the year's midpoint, it's a prime time to assess our daily operations. Are we functioning at peak efficiency? Or are there creases in our workflows that need ironing out? Let's focus on enhancing productivity this month, ensuring that our business operations are as smooth and efficient as they can be.

Week 1: Self-Audit & Research
- Day 1-2: Conduct a thorough review of your daily tasks. List them out, and note which ones consume the most time.
- Day 3-4: Identify bottlenecks or repetitive tasks. Are there any tasks you dread? Those might be prime candidates for streamlining.
- Day 5-6: Research productivity tools. There are myriad out there – from task management to automated marketing.
- Day 7: Speak to peers or industry leaders. Learn about the tools or strategies they employ for enhanced productivity.

Week 2: Implementation & Training
- Day 8-9: Choose a tool or software that you think will best address your needs. Begin the implementation process.
- Day 10-12: If it's a tool that requires team usage, conduct a training session. Ensure everyone is comfortable with the new system.
- Day 13-14: Slowly integrate this tool into your daily operations. Start by using it for just one or two tasks.

Week 3: Monitoring & Adjustments
- Day 15-16: Track your progress. Has the new tool or change made a tangible difference in your workflow?

- Day 17-18: Gather feedback from your team. Are they finding it easier or encountering any challenges?
- Day 19-21: Based on the feedback and your observations, make necessary adjustments. Remember, the goal is streamlined operations.

Week 4: Expansion & Refinement
- Day 22-23: Consider expanding the tool's usage to other areas of your operations.
- Day 24-25: Look into advanced features or plugins that could offer even greater efficiency.
- Day 26-28: Dedicate time to refining the process, ensuring all kinks are ironed out.
- Day 29-30: Reflect on the month's changes. Prepare a report comparing your efficiency levels before and after the changes.

Bonus Activities:
- Efficiency Workshop: Consider hosting an efficiency workshop where team members can share personal productivity tips.
- Productivity Challenge: Start a fun challenge where team members compete to showcase the most effective productivity hacks they employ in their roles.

June is about optimizing your business operations, ensuring every moment counts. A business that constantly strives for efficiency is not only poised for growth but also creates a satisfying and productive environment for its team. Here's to a smarter, more streamlined June!

July Challenge

Ah, July! As the sun blazes in its full glory and the days stretch out, we find ourselves at the midpoint of the year. It's the perfect moment to hit the pause button, take a step back, and evaluate our journey thus far. A mid-year review allows us to recalibrate, celebrate our wins, and make strategic shifts where necessary. Ready to dive in?

Week 1: Personal Reflection & Data Collection
- Day 1-2: Begin with a personal reflection. Revisit your goals from January. Note your emotions, successes, and any roadblocks.
- Day 3-4: Collect quantitative data. This could include financial statements, sales figures, website traffic stats, and other relevant metrics.
- Day 5-6: Speak informally with your team members. Gauge their feelings about the past six months.
- Day 7: Organize and categorize your collected data for easy analysis.

Week 2: Analysis & Team Feedback
- Day 8-9: Analyze the quantitative data. Compare it against the targets or benchmarks you'd set for yourself.
- Day 10-11: Hold feedback sessions with your team. Understand their perspective on what went well and what could be improved.
- Day 12-14: Synthesize personal reflections, quantitative data, and team feedback. Look for patterns or recurring themes.

Week 3: Strategy Adjustments & New Initiatives
- Day 15-16: Based on your insights from the previous weeks, identify areas that require strategic adjustments.

- Day 17-18: Plan new initiatives or campaigns that address the identified gaps or opportunities.
- Day 19-20: Initiate the changes on a small scale to test their effectiveness.
- Day 21: Document the new strategies and communicate any major shifts to relevant stakeholders.

Week 4: Preparations for the Latter Half
- Day 22-23: Set clear, actionable goals for the next six months. Be realistic yet challenging.
- Day 24-25: Allocate resources, both human and financial, to your new initiatives.
- Day 26-28: Encourage team members to set their personal and professional goals for the remainder of the year.
- Day 29-30: Celebrate the month's insights and learnings. Maybe throw a small party or have a team-building day!

Bonus Activities:
- Peer Review Sessions: Implement a system where team members can offer constructive feedback to each other.
- Visualization Tools: Use tools like mind maps or vision boards to visually represent the next phase of your business journey.

July provides a pivotal checkpoint in our year-long journey. With a thoughtful review process, we equip ourselves with the knowledge and insights to power through the remaining months with clarity and purpose. Let this month's review set the stage for even more significant achievements in the months to come!

August Challenge

August is synonymous with the warm zenith of summer, and much like nature in full bloom, it's a month beckoning your business to flourish and evolve. With more than half the year behind us, now is the time to channel your inner innovator and push the boundaries of what's possible. Expanding and innovating doesn't always mean going big; sometimes, it's the subtle tweaks and enhancements that lead to the most profound impact. Ready to elevate your entrepreneurial game? Let's dive into the month of growth!

Week 1: Feedback & Market Analysis
- Day 1-2: Kick off the month by gathering recent feedback from your customers. Use surveys, feedback forms, or even casual conversations.
- Day 3-4: Dive into market analysis. Identify trends, emerging technologies, or shifts in consumer behavior.
- Day 5-6: Analyze competitor movements. Any new offerings or strategies they've recently introduced?
- Day 7: Synthesize all the information. Identify gaps in your offerings or areas ripe for innovation.

Week 2: Ideation & Brainstorming
- Day 8-9: Organize focused brainstorming sessions. Encourage free-thinking and wild ideas.
- Day 10-11: Explore collaborative ideation. Maybe involve some of your loyal customers or partners in the brainstorming.
- Day 12-14: Prioritize ideas. Which of them align best with your brand, resources, and market demand?

Week 3: Prototype & Validation
- Day 15-17: Choose one or two top ideas and create a prototype or a basic version.

- Day 18-19: Share the prototype with a select group of customers or stakeholders. Gather initial reactions.
- Day 20-21: Refine the idea based on feedback. Consider feasibility, costs, and potential return on investment.

Week 4: Implementation & Launch
- Day 22-24: Develop a rollout plan. This could involve marketing strategies, production timelines, or training sessions for your team.
- Day 25-26: Soft launch your innovation, perhaps to a segmented audience or region.
- Day 27-29: Collect data on the reception. Is it meeting expectations? Any unforeseen challenges?
- Day 30-31: Based on feedback and initial results, make final tweaks and plan for a broader launch.

Bonus Activities:
- Shadowing Sessions: Spend a day shadowing a team member or even a customer to gain fresh perspectives.
- Innovation Journals: Encourage your team to maintain journals capturing daily insights, which can be goldmines for future innovations.

August, with its vibe of growth and rejuvenation, is the ideal time to introduce fresh vigor into your business. By embracing innovation, you're not just adding a new feature or service; you're ensuring your business stays relevant, competitive, and ever-evolving in the marketplace. Here's to the exciting changes August can bring to your entrepreneurial journey!

September Challenge

As the amber hues of September roll in and signal the transition from summer to autumn, there's no better time to turn your focus inward and refine your skills. Just as nature prepares for the season ahead, equipping yourself with new skills or sharpening existing ones can fortify your business against future challenges. Every entrepreneur knows that knowledge is not static; the learning curve is continuous. This month, challenge yourself to evolve, learn, and step up your game in areas that can set you apart in the entrepreneurial world.

Week 1: Self-Assessment & Goal Setting
- Day 1-2: Reflect on your current skill set. Where do you excel? Where could you improve?
- Day 3-4: Set clear objectives. What do you wish to learn or improve upon by the end of the month?
- Day 5-6: Research available resources. This could be online courses, local workshops, or seminars in your area.
- Day 7: Enroll in your chosen course or workshop. Mark the start and end dates on your calendar.

Week 2: Dive into Learning
- Day 8-10: Dedicate focused hours to your course or workshop. Take notes and actively participate in discussions.
- Day 11-13: Practice what you've learned so far. Real-world application will reinforce your learning.
- Day 14: Reflect on your progress. Adjust your learning pace if necessary.

Week 3: Mastering & Application
- Day 15-17: Continue your course or workshop. Start thinking about how you can apply these new skills to your business.

- Day 18-20: Implement the skills in a real-world scenario. Perhaps a project or a task that can benefit from your new knowledge.
- Day 21: Gather feedback. How did your new skills impact the outcome?

Week 4: Sharing & Consolidation
- Day 22-23: Review and consolidate your learnings. Create a reference guide or notes that you can revisit.
- Day 24-26: Plan and prepare your own workshop or webinar. Outline the content, decide on the format, and pick a date.
- Day 27-29: Promote your workshop or webinar. Invite your network, colleagues, or customers.
- Day 30: Host your event. Share your knowledge, engage with participants, and enjoy the process of giving back.

Bonus Activities:
- Mentorship: Consider seeking a mentor in the area of your skill development. Their experience can offer invaluable insights.
- Skill Swap: Partner with a fellow entrepreneur to teach each other a new skill. It's a win-win!

September, with its essence of change and renewal, serves as the perfect backdrop for personal and professional growth. By investing in your skills, you're investing in the future of your business. Remember, learning is an ongoing journey, and every new skill acquired is a powerful tool in your entrepreneurial arsenal. Cheers to a September of growth, learning, and empowerment!

October Challenge

As the golden leaves of October fall and the world prepares for the end of the year, there's a certain tranquility in the air that beckons for reflection and self-care. The pace of modern life, especially for entrepreneurs, can often be frantic, with digital devices constantly buzzing with notifications, calls, and endless streams of information. This month, the challenge is to disconnect to reconnect. By allowing ourselves to take a step back from the digital world, we can gain clarity, rejuvenate our mental health, and recharge our energy. Enjoy an October that's more about introspection and less about Instagram.

Week 1: Awareness & Preparation
- Day 1-2: Track your screen time. Note down how many hours you spend on different apps and devices.
- Day 3-4: Reflect on the data. Identify which apps or activities are taking most of your time.
- Day 5-6: Set your detox goals. Determine how long your detox will be and what you aim to achieve from it.
- Day 7: Inform colleagues, friends, or clients about your upcoming digital detox to set expectations.

Week 2: The Digital Detox Weekend
- Day 8: Prepare your environment. Create a clutter-free space. Perhaps introduce calming elements like candles or soft music.
- Day 9-10: Begin your detox. Engage in activities that don't involve screens – read a physical book, go for a nature walk, meditate, or try a new hobby.
- Day 11: Reflect on the detox experience. How did you feel? What did you notice about your mood and energy levels?
- Day 12-14: Slowly reintroduce devices, but with mindful usage. Limit checking emails or social media to specific times of the day.

Week 3: Implementing Daily Detox Hours
- Day 15-17: Choose an hour each day for a mini digital detox. This could be during lunch or before bedtime.
- Day 18-20: Engage in non-digital activities during this hour. This could be journaling, drawing, cooking, or simply relaxing.
- Day 21: Reflect on the impact of daily detox hours. Do you feel more present? Is your sleep pattern improving?

Week 4: Solidifying Habits & Looking Ahead
- Day 22-24: Evaluate the tools and apps you use. Uninstall or reduce notifications for apps that aren't essential.
- Day 25-26: Set boundaries for work-related device usage. For instance, no checking emails after 7 PM.
- Day 27-29: Share your experience. Consider writing a blog post or social media update about your digital detox journey.
- Day 30: Plan your next detox. Monthly, quarterly, or yearly – decide when your next digital break will be.

Bonus Activities:
- Tech-Free Zones: Designate certain areas of your home as tech-free zones, like the dining room or bedroom.
- Physical Activities: Incorporate physical activities like yoga or dance that require you to be present and in the moment.

October, with its gentle reminders of nature's cycles, offers the perfect setting for your own cycle of rejuvenation. Embrace the month with an intention to find balance between the digital world and the tangible, beautiful world around you. As you unplug from the matrix, you might just find that you plug more deeply into your own well-being, creativity, and peace. Here's to an October filled with digital clarity and personal growth!

November Challenge

As November unfolds, bringing with it the crispness of fall and the anticipation of winter, it's a month where we're naturally reminded of the things we're thankful for. Gratitude isn't just an emotion; it's a practice that, when cultivated, can lead to deeper connections, increased happiness, and a more fulfilled life. For entrepreneurs, it's also an opportunity to infuse your business with purpose and meaning. By focusing on gratitude and giving back, businesses can foster positive change in the community while also building a loyal and engaged customer base. Let this November be the month where your business stands for more than just profit – where it stands for purpose.

Week 1: Understanding Gratitude
- Day 1-2: Start a gratitude journal. Every day, write down three things you're grateful for in your business journey.
- Day 3-4: Share your gratitude. Post on your business's social about a customer, employee, or partner you're thankful for.
- Day 5-6: Reflect on challenges. Recognize a past difficulty and find aspects of it to be thankful for – perhaps it taught you resilience or introduced you to a mentor.
- Day 7: Engage with your audience. Encourage them to share what they're grateful for, building community around positivity.

Week 2: Identifying Causes
- Day 8-9: Research local charities or global causes that resonate with your business values.
- Day 10: Engage your team or audience in a poll to select a charitable initiative to support.
- Day 11-13: Plan out a giving strategy. Will you donate a portion of profits, offer your products/services, or perhaps volunteer time?

- Day 14: Announce your chosen cause and your plans to support it through your business platform.

Week 3: Taking Action
- Day 15-16: Kick off your charitable initiative. Promote it actively across all channels.
- Day 17-18: Engage in community service. If possible, close shop for half a day and rally your team to volunteer locally.
- Day 19-21: Share the journey. Post updates, pictures, or testimonials showcasing the impact of the initiative. This isn't about bragging but about inspiring others to join.

Week 4: Cultivating a Culture of Giving
- Day 22-24: Encourage your team to share their personal stories of giving & volunteering. Recognize & celebrate them.
- Day 25: Host a workshop or seminar on the importance of community involvement and corporate responsibility.
- Day 26-28: Set up a long-term giving strategy. Consider starting a monthly or quarterly giving tradition.
- Day 29-30: Reflect on the month's activities. Gather feedback from the team, customers, and the supported charity. Use this to guide future giving initiatives.

Bonus Activities:
- Gratitude Wall: Set up a board in your office where team members can post sticky notes of gratitude.
- Matched Giving: Motivate your employees by matching their personal charitable donations.

November, with its intrinsic theme of thanksgiving, offers a golden chance to make giving an integral part of your business DNA. This isn't about a one-off charitable act but fostering a genuine culture of gratitude and giving that extends beyond this month.

December Challenge

December, cloaked in its festive spirit and wintry charm, beckons not just the close of a year but also a moment for deep introspection. It's a month where the lines between reflection and celebration blur. As entrepreneurs, the temptation to simply dive into the next year's planning can be immense. But pausing, taking stock, and genuinely recharging is paramount. Before the new year's hustle takes over, December provides a sanctuary to look back, appreciate the journey, and mentally rejuvenate. In this month, let your business bask in the warmth of accomplishments and lessons alike, gearing up for yet another year of adventures.

Week 1: Yearly Recap
- Day 1-2: Dedicate time to list out the year's major accomplishments, big or small.
- Day 3-4: Reflect on the challenges faced. What did they teach you? How did they shape your business?
- Day 5: Celebrate the team. Share the yearly recap with them, acknowledging their efforts.
- Day 6-7: Share the recap with your customers and stakeholders, thanking them for being a part of the journey.

Week 2: Dive into the Details
- Day 8-9: Deep dive into financials. How did your revenue, profits, and expenses fare against the forecasts?
- Day 10-11: Assess your marketing and sales efforts. Which campaigns worked? Which didn't?
- Day 12-13: Review customer feedback and testimonials. What can you improve?
- Day 14: Gather the team for feedback. What can be improved in the working environment, processes, or strategies?

Week 3: Planning Ahead
- Day 15-16: Set the tone for the next year. What's the overarching theme or primary objective?
- Day 17-18: Brainstorm product or service launches for the upcoming year.
- Day 19: Plan out potential marketing strategies or campaigns.
- Day 20-21: Identify areas of skill development or training required for you or your team.

Week 4: Recharging for the New Year
- Day 22-23: Declutter your workspace. A clean environment can lead to a clear mind.
- Day 24: Hold a team celebration. It could be a party, dinner, or even a simple virtual hangout.
- Day 25: Take a day off. Completely. No emails, no work.
- Day 26-28: Dedicate some time for personal self-care. This could be reading, spa sessions, or just lazying around.
- Day 29-31: Set your intentions. Visualize the upcoming year and the successes you wish to achieve.

Bonus Activities:
- Gratitude Jar: Throughout the month, encourage team members to write down things they're thankful for and put them in a jar. Read them out in the new year's first meeting.
- Vision Board: Create a vision board for the next year, visualizing your goals and aspirations.

December, with its gentle reminders of the transient nature of time, is the perfect backdrop for such introspection and rejuvenation. As entrepreneurs, understanding the balance between relentless pursuit and restful reflection is crucial. This month is not just about planning the next year's ascent but also cherishing the altitude already achieved.

Monthly Journal Prompts

Journaling can be an entrepreneur's secret weapon. It provides an avenue for introspection, idea generation, and emotional release. Here's a monthly guide with specific prompts to help channel your thoughts and foster growth throughout the year.

January: Beginnings & Intentions
- What are my primary goals for this year? Why are they important to me?
- What did I learn from the previous year that I can apply now?
- How do I want to feel at the end of this month, and what steps can help me achieve that feeling?

February: Love & Passion
- What am I most passionate about in my business?
- How can I bring more love and care into my work?
- How can I show appreciation to myself and my team this month?

March: Growth & Expansion
- What new areas am I looking to explore or expand into?
- Are there any fears holding me back? How can I address them?
- What feedback have I received that can help me grow?

April: Renewal & Energy
- As nature blooms, how can I inject new energy into my ventures?
- Are there any stale areas or methods in my business that need refreshing?
- What excites me most about the upcoming quarter?

May: Gratitude & Abundance
- List five things in my business journey I'm genuinely thankful for.
- How can I cultivate a mindset of abundance rather than scarcity?
- What are the little wins this month I can celebrate?

June: Mid-Year Reflection
- Am I on track with my goals? If not, what adjustments are needed?
- What unexpected challenges or opportunities have surfaced? How have I responded?
- How has my vision for the year evolved?

July: Balance & Rest
- How am I ensuring a balance between hustle and rest?
- What activities rejuvenate me outside of work?
- Are there any areas where I'm feeling burned out, and how can I address them?

August: Courage & Challenges
- What challenges am I currently facing, and how can I overcome them?
- When did I last step out of my comfort zone?
- What would I attempt if I knew I could not fail?

September: Learning & Development
- What new skills or knowledge have I acquired or wish to pursue?
- How have I grown as a leader and entrepreneur?
- Are there any courses, workshops, or books I want to delve into?

October: Creativity & Innovation
- How can I foster a more creative environment in my workspace?
- Are there new, innovative strategies I wish to explore?
- When did I last feel truly inspired, and how can I recreate such moments?

November: Giving & Community
- How is my business positively impacting the community or world at large?
- In what ways can I give back, whether in time, resources, or mentorship?
- What legacy do I wish to create?

December: Reflection & Celebration
- What are my top three achievements this year?
- How have I grown personally and professionally?
- As the year closes, what are my hopes and aspirations for the next one?

Remember, there's no right or wrong way to journal. Embrace the process, be honest with yourself, and let these prompts guide you through a year filled with growth, discovery, and success.

Business Planning Template

Executive Summary:
- Business Name:
- Business Description:
- Mission Statement:
- Vision Statement:
- Objectives:

Market Analysis:
- Target Audience:
- Market Needs:
- Market Trends:
- Competition:

Operational Plan:
- Location:
- Suppliers:
- Equipment/Tools:
- Staffing Needs:

Financial Projections:
- Start-up Costs:
- Monthly Operating Costs:
- Projected Revenue:
- Break-even Analysis:

SWOT Analysis:
- Strengths:
- Weaknesses:
- Opportunities:
- Threats:

Monthly Budgeting Worksheet

A. INCOME

1. Product/Service Sales:
- Product A: _____
- Product B: _____
(Continue listing all services)
2. Other Income:
- Affiliate income: _____
- Royalties: _____
- Partnership revenues: _____
- Miscellaneous: _____

Total Income (A): _____

B. FIXED COSTS

1. Rent/Mortgage:
- Business premise rent: _____
- Storage rent: _____
2. Utilities:
- Electricity: _____
- Water: _____
- Internet: _____
- Phone: _____
3. Salaries:
- Management: _____
- Full-time staff: _____
- Part-time staff: _____
- Overtime: _____

4. Insurance:
- Property insurance: _____
- Health insurance: _____
- Business liability insurance: _____
- Workers compensation: _____

5. Others (Fixed):
- Software subscriptions: _____
- Licensing/royalties: _____
- Professional fees (Accountant, Lawyer): _____
- Office supplies (Stationery): _____

Total Fixed Costs (B): _____

C. VARIABLE COSTS

1. Marketing & Advertising:
- Digital ads (e.g., Facebook, Google): _____
- Print ads: _____
- Influencer collaborations: _____
- Event sponsorships: _____

2. Supplies:
- Raw materials: _____
- Packaging: _____

3. Shipping:
- Domestic: _____
- International: _____
- Returns processing: _____

4. Others (Variable):
- Travel & entertainment: _____
- Training & development: _____
- Maintenance/Repairs: _____
- Miscellaneous expenses: _____

Total Variable Costs (C): _____

D. MONTHLY TOTALS

1. Total Income (A): _____

2. Total Fixed Costs (B): _____

3. Total Variable Costs (C): _____

Net Income (A - B - C): _____

Workbook Challenges

1. Vision & Goal Setting
Exercise: Create Your Vision Statement
- Write down what you envision for your business in the next five years. Think about your company's culture, its size, market position, and any other elements that come to mind.
- Reflection: Why is this vision important to you?

Exercise: SMART Goals Breakdown
- Using the SMART criteria (Specific, Measurable, Achievable, Relevant, Time-bound), break down your primary business goal for the year.
- Action: Assign deadlines to each step of your goal.

2. Financial Fitness
Exercise: Cost Analysis
- List down three expenses that you feel could be reduced and explore alternative options for them.
- Reflection: How will cutting these costs impact your business in the short and long term?

Exercise: Revenue Streams Brainstorm
- Identify any potential new revenue streams for your business.
- Action: Pick one and draft a preliminary plan to implement.

3. Marketing Mastery
Exercise: Customer Profile
- Create a detailed profile of your ideal customer. Consider demographics, psychographics, and buying behaviors.
- Reflection: How can you tailor your marketing to appeal specifically to this customer?

Exercise: Marketing SWOT Analysis
- Conduct a SWOT analysis (Strengths, Weaknesses, Opportunities, Threats) of your current marketing strategy.
- Action: Identify one strength to capitalize on and one weakness to improve.

4. Network & Expand
Exercise: Elevator Pitch Practice
- Write down and refine your business's elevator pitch.
- Action: Test your pitch on someone unfamiliar with your business and gather feedback.

Exercise: Collaboration Brainstorm
- List potential businesses or individuals you could collaborate with and how it would benefit both parties.
- Action: Reach out to one of them with a collaboration proposal.

5. Customer Appreciation
Exercise: Feedback Loop
- Design a system or survey to gather feedback from your customers.
- Reflection: Analyze the feedback from the last month and identify areas of improvement.

Exercise: Loyalty Program Blueprint
- Sketch out a basic loyalty program or a referral program for your business.
- Action: Implement a small aspect of it and measure its success.

6. Productivity & Efficiency
Exercise: Time Tracking
- Track how you spend your working hours for a week.
- Reflection: Identify any time wasters and think about how you can eliminate or reduce them.

Exercise: Process Mapping
- Map out the process for a common task in your business.
- Action: Streamline one part of that process and implement the change.

As you navigate through these steps, remember that the entrepreneurial journey is unique for everyone. Here are some pointers to ensure you make the most of these exercises:

- Consistency is Key: Dedicate time regularly to work through these sections. Whether it's a set time each week or just a few moments when you can spare them, consistency will help embed these practices into your daily routine.
- Embrace the Reflection: Some of the most valuable insights come from self-reflection. Don't rush through the reflective parts of the exercises; give yourself the grace and space to think deeply.
- Celebrate Small Wins: The journey of building a business is made up of small, incremental steps. Celebrate the small victories along the way. They accumulate and pave the path to your larger goals.
- Seek Feedback: Share your insights, goals, or plans from these exercises with a mentor, business partner, or fellow entrepreneur. They might offer a fresh perspective or valuable advice.
- Revisit Often: Your goals, challenges, and business environment may change. Revisiting these workbook sections can offer new insights or remind you of foundational principles when faced with new challenges.

Daily Habits

Success isn't just about grand gestures or monumental decisions. Often, it's the little things we do each day that contribute to our long-term achievements. Over the years, many successful women entrepreneurs have credited their daily routines and habits as significant factors behind their success. Let's explore some of these habits to gain inspiration and insights:

1. Morning Rituals: Starting the day right can set the tone for everything that follows. Many successful women swear by a morning routine. This could involve meditation, journaling, exercise, or simply some quiet time with a cup of tea.

2. Prioritization: Knowing what's essential and what can wait is a skill in itself. Successful women often begin their day by listing their top three most crucial tasks and ensuring they tackle them.

3. Continuous Learning: Whether it's reading a book, taking an online course, or attending workshops, the quest for knowledge is never-ending. Setting aside even just 20 minutes a day for learning can make a difference.

4. Time Management: Time blocks, the Pomodoro technique, or the two-minute rule; finding a time management strategy that works for you can boost productivity immeasurably.

5. Self-care: All work and no play isn't the mantra here. Regular breaks, mindfulness practices, and hobbies outside of work help in recharging and maintaining a work-life balance.

6. Networking: Building and maintaining relationships is essential in the business world. Successful women make it a habit to reach out, connect, and engage with their network regularly.

7. Gratitude Practice: Whether it's a dedicated gratitude journal or a few moments of reflection at the end of the day, acknowledging the good can foster a positive mindset.

8. Setting Boundaries: Knowing when to say no, when to step back, and when to delegate are all crucial for maintaining sanity and ensuring the quality of work.

9. Visualizing Success: Taking a few minutes daily to visualize goals, aspirations, and success scenarios can be a powerful motivator and clarifier.

10. Feedback and Reflection: Regularly assessing one's performance, seeking feedback, and making necessary adjustments is a habit that keeps many women entrepreneurs on top of their game.

It's worth noting that while these habits have worked for many, the key is to find what works best for you. Personalize these habits, experiment with them, and make them your own. The daily habits you cultivate can act as the foundation upon which you build your empire.

Elevator Pitch Builder

The elevator pitch is the business world's version of a first impression. In a matter of seconds, you must convey the essence, value, and potential of your business idea. Whether you're at a networking event, seeking a potential investor, or simply explaining what you do at a family gathering, a well-crafted elevator pitch can open doors.

Why is an Elevator Pitch Important?
1. First Impressions: You only get one chance at a first impression; make it count.
2. Clarity of Thought: Being able to succinctly describe your business demonstrates clarity of thought and purpose.
3. Opportunity: You never know where a chance meeting could lead. Be prepared for serendipity.

Key Elements of a Strong Elevator Pitch:
1. Problem: Clearly state the problem or need your business addresses.
2. Solution: Describe how your product or service provides a solution.
3. Target Market: Define who will benefit from your solution.
4. Unique Selling Proposition (USP): What makes your business stand out from the competition?
5. Call to Action: If appropriate, include a brief call to action – what do you want the listener to do next?

Steps to Craft Your Elevator Pitch:
1. Start with Why: Before the 'what' and 'how', start with the 'why' of your business. Why does your business exist, and why should anyone care?

2. Be Concise: Remember, an elevator pitch is typically between 30 to 60 seconds. Trim the fat and get to the point.
3. Practice: Once you've drafted your pitch, practice it. Refine it based on feedback, and ensure it sounds natural, not rehearsed.
4. Adapt: While you should have a standard pitch, be prepared to tweak it based on the audience or situation.
5. Engage with a Question: Ending with a question can engage the listener and spark a conversation.

Sample Elevator Pitch:
"Did you know that 70% of smartphone users experience eye strain from prolonged use? Our app, 'EyeGuard', adjusts screen settings in real-time based on ambient light and usage patterns to reduce eye fatigue. We're focusing on the health-conscious segment of smartphone users. Unlike other screen dimming apps, ours uses AI to predict and adjust settings, ensuring optimal screen conditions at all times. Would you be interested in trying it out?"

Tips for a Memorable Pitch:
1. Passion is Infectious: Let your passion for your business shine through.
2. Avoid Jargon: Make sure your pitch is understandable to anyone, regardless of their familiarity with your industry.
3. Tell a Story: People remember stories better than facts. If appropriate, weave a brief story into your pitch.
4. Stay Positive: Focus on the positive aspects and potential of your business.

Perfecting your elevator pitch takes time and iteration. However, once mastered, it becomes a potent tool in your entrepreneurial toolkit, ready to help you seize opportunities whenever they arise.

Networking Tips

In the realm of business, a robust network can be your most potent asset. Whether you're seeking clients, partnerships, investors, or simply expanding your horizons, networking is a critical tool for success. The adage "It's not just what you know, but who you know" rings true for a reason.

Why is Networking Essential?
1. Opportunities: Networking can open doors to job opportunities, partnerships, or new market areas.
2. Knowledge Exchange: Gain insights, feedback, or advice from those who've been there, done that.
3. Increased Visibility: Regular networking can increase your brand's visibility in the market.
4. Mentorship: Establishing relationships can lead to mentorship, an invaluable resource for growth.
5. Friendship: Beyond professional gains, networking can lead to meaningful, lasting friendships.

Effective Networking Strategies:
1. Quality Over Quantity: Building deeper, meaningful connections is more valuable than accumulating a plethora of superficial contacts.
2. Listen Actively: Networking isn't just about talking; it's about listening. Be genuinely interested in what others have to say.
3. Offer Value: Instead of approaching networking from a "what can I get?" perspective, think "what can I offer?"
4. Follow Up: Meeting someone once won't establish a lasting connection. Make it a point to follow up and nurture relationships.

5. Diversify Your Networks: Engage in various events, groups, and platforms to meet people from different industries and backgrounds.

Networking in the Digital Age:
1. Leverage Social Media: Platforms like LinkedIn, Twitter, and industry-specific forums can be goldmines for networking. Engage in discussions, share insights, and connect with industry peers.
2. Webinars and Online Events: Attend online conferences, workshops, or seminars. They often offer networking breakout sessions.
3. Maintain a Professional Online Persona: Ensure your online profiles are up-to-date and resonate with the professional image you want to project.

Networking Tips for Introverts:
1. One-on-One Meetings: If large events feel overwhelming, opt for individual meetings or smaller group settings.
2. Prepare Questions: Having a set of questions can act as a conversation starter and ease initial discomfort.
3. Set Achievable Goals: Instead of aiming to talk to ten people at an event, start with two or three.
4. Find Common Ground: Finding mutual interests can make conversations more engaging and less taxing.

The Etiquette of Networking:
1. Be Authentic: People appreciate genuine interest and honesty. Avoid overselling yourself.
2. Respect Boundaries: Understand when to step back. If someone seems disinterested, don't push.
3. Stay Organized: Keep track of whom you meet. A simple CRM tool or even a spreadsheet can help.

4. Thank Before and After: Send a brief thank-you note after meeting someone. Express gratitude for their time and insights.

Remember, while networking is a professional endeavor, it's rooted in human relationships. Be kind, be curious, and be genuine. As you sow the seeds of trust and mutual respect, you'll see your network blossom, bringing myriad opportunities and rewards.

The Social Breakdown

In today's digital era, establishing a presence on social media platforms is imperative. However, it's essential to pick the right platforms based on your business type, target audience, and objectives. Here's a breakdown of the top social media platforms and insights to guide your choices:

1. Facebook

- Primary Demographics: 18-49-year-olds, slightly skewed towards women.
- Best For: B2C businesses, e-commerce, local businesses, news & entertainment.
- Business Insights:
  - Engage with Facebook Groups to tap into niche communities.
  - Utilize Facebook Marketplace for selling products.
  - Facebook Ads allow for detailed targeting based on interests and behaviors.

2. Instagram

- Primary Demographics: 18-35-year-olds, predominantly female.
- Best For: Fashion, travel, arts, e-commerce, and lifestyle brands.
- Business Insights:
  - Instagram Stories & Reels provide an engaging medium to reach the audience.
  - Collaborate with influencers for product promotions.
  - Use IGTV for longer video content.

3. YouTube

- Primary Demographics: 18-44-year-olds, evenly split between genders.
- Best For: Any business that benefits from video content – tutorials, product launches, behind-the-scenes.
- Business Insights:
  - SEO is crucial: Optimize video titles, descriptions, and tags.
  - Engage with your community in the comments.
  - Collaborate with YouTubers for joint content.

4. TikTok

- Primary Demographics: 16-24-year-olds, slightly skewed towards women.
- Best For: Brands targeting Gen Z, fashion, music, lifestyle, and entertainment.
- Business Insights:
  - Keep content fun, engaging, and in line with current trends.
  - Challenges and hashtag campaigns can go viral.
  - TikTok ads are a powerful way to target Gen Z.

5. Pinterest

- Primary Demographics: 18-49-year-olds, predominantly female.
- Best For: DIY, fashion, recipes, wedding planning, home decor, and e-commerce.
- Business Insights:
  - Rich Pins provide more information about pinned images (e.g., price of a product).
  - The platform drives significant referral traffic to websites.
  - Collaborate with top pinners to amplify your reach.

6. Twitter (now X)

- Primary Demographics: 18-29-year-olds, a balanced gender split.
- Best For: News outlets, writers, public figures, tech companies.
- Business Insights:
  - Engage in real-time events and trending topics.
  - Twitter Chats can help engage with your community.
  - Use Twitter Ads for promotions.

7. LinkedIn

- Primary Demographics: 25-45-year-olds, professionals across industries.
- Best For: B2B, recruiters, educational institutions, professionals offering services.
- Business Insights:
  - LinkedIn articles can position you as an industry thought leader.
  - LinkedIn Ads target professionals based on their job title, industry, etc.
  - Engage with LinkedIn Groups to tap into specific industries or niches.

Selecting the right platform(s) is based on where your target audience hangs out and the nature of your product or service. Regularly review platform analytics to understand engagement and ROI. Always be prepared to adapt and evolve as platforms change and as your business grows. The social media landscape is dynamic, and agility will keep you at the forefront.

Event Planning

Whether you're launching a product, hosting a workshop, or celebrating another significant business milestone, executing a successful event requires meticulous planning. This checklist aims to streamline your event planning process and ensure you cover all bases:

1. Define Event Objectives:
- What's the purpose? (e.g., product launch, networking, workshop)
- Who's your target audience?
- What do you hope to achieve? (e.g., sales, leads, brand awareness)

2. Set a Budget:
- Venue rental
- Catering and refreshments
- Entertainment or guest speakers
- Marketing and promotion
- Equipment rental (AV equipment, chairs, etc.)
- Miscellaneous expenses (decor, giveaways, etc.)

3. Choose a Date and Venue:
- Ensure it doesn't clash with major holidays or industry events.
- Consider venue location, capacity, parking, and facilities.
- Book well in advance and secure any necessary permits.

4. Plan Logistics:
- Floor layout and seating arrangement
- Equipment setup (microphones, projectors, etc.)
- Signage for directing guests
- Emergency exit routes

5. Secure Speakers or Entertainment:
- Confirm their availability and fees.
- Prepare a run-of-show or itinerary.
- Conduct rehearsals if necessary.

6. Marketing and Promotion:
- Create an event page or website.
- Promote through email campaigns, social media, and local press.
- Offer early bird discounts or promotions.

7. Prepare Materials:
- Event programs or itineraries
- Name tags or badges
- Presentation slides or videos
- Product samples, if applicable

8. Coordinate with Vendors:
- Catering and menu selection
- Equipment rentals
- Decor and theme planning

9. Manage RSVPs and Registrations:
- Use online platforms for ticket sales or reservations.
- Keep a database of attendees for follow-up.

10. Plan for the Unexpected:
- Have a backup plan for outdoor events (e.g., tents for rain).
- Prepare a first aid kit and emergency contacts.
- Ensure there's a plan for security or crowd management.

11. Execute with Finesse:
- Brief your team on event day roles.

- Ensure timely setup and teardown.
- Engage with attendees and gather feedback.

12. Post-Event Actions:
- Send thank-you notes or emails to attendees, speakers, and sponsors.
- Analyze the event's success and areas of improvement.
- Document learnings for future events.

Event planning requires foresight, attention to detail, and flexibility. Use this checklist as a starting point, but always be prepared to adapt based on the unique needs of your event and business. Here's to hosting a memorable event that amplifies your business goals!

Guided Meditation

Finding Your Business Zen

Begin by finding a comfortable seated position. Close your eyes and take a deep breath, inhaling positivity and exhaling any doubts or fears.

Imagine a serene place, perhaps a garden or a quiet room filled with soft light. As you enter this space, you see a table with a crystal-clear bowl filled with water. This bowl represents your business. Notice how calm the water is.

Now, imagine dropping a pebble into this bowl, creating gentle ripples. Each ripple represents an action, decision, or choice in your business. Visualize these ripples expanding outward, touching every aspect of your entrepreneurial journey, from your clients to your team.

Allow yourself to feel the energy and momentum each ripple creates. Trust in the process, knowing that with each action, you're creating positive change.

Take another deep breath and open your eyes, ready to embrace the day's challenges with renewed energy.

Overcoming Entrepreneurial Anxiety

Sit comfortably, close your eyes, and focus on your breath. Inhale deeply, filling your lungs, and exhale slowly, releasing any tension.

Picture yourself on a mountain peak, looking down at a vast landscape. This landscape represents the journey of your business. Notice the valleys, the high peaks, and the winding paths.

Each valley symbolizes challenges, while the peaks represent your successes. The winding paths are your unique journey through entrepreneurship.

Now, focus on one of the valleys. See it not as a setback but as a lesson, an opportunity for growth. With each breath, transform this valley into a gentle hill, making it easier to cross.

As you breathe out, release any fear or anxiety, knowing that each challenge only brings you closer to your next peak.

Take one final deep breath, feeling empowered and ready to face any obstacle on your entrepreneurial path. Slowly open your eyes.

Utilizing these meditation scripts can offer a mental break and shift your perspective, helping you approach your business with a clearer, more focused mind. Embrace them during moments of doubt or when seeking motivation, grounding yourself in the present and reaffirming your entrepreneurial spirit.

Managing Burnout

Burnout isn't just a buzzword; it's a genuine phenomenon that many entrepreneurs face at various stages of their journey. It's that feeling of mental, emotional, and sometimes physical exhaustion, often combined with doubts about your competence and the value of your work. When burnout strikes, it can reduce creativity, hinder performance, and lead to health problems. Here's how to tackle it head-on:

1. Recognize the Signs
The first step in dealing with burnout is recognizing it. Symptoms can vary but often include:
- Constant fatigue
- Decreased motivation
- Feelings of cynicism or detachment
- Reduced performance

2. Set Clear Boundaries
As an entrepreneur, it's tempting to always be "on." However, continuous availability can quickly lead to burnout. Set strict working hours and let your team, clients, and partners know these boundaries. This might mean no business emails or calls after 7 PM or dedicating weekends strictly to personal time. By doing so, you create a mental separation between work and rest.

3. Prioritize Self-Care
Beyond setting boundaries, ensure you're allocating time for activities that rejuvenate your mind, body, and spirit. This could be reading, exercise, spending time with loved ones, or even just a long, uninterrupted nap.

4. Learn to Delegate
You might feel the need to control every aspect of your business, but delegating tasks – especially those outside your expertise or those that are repetitive – can significantly reduce feelings of overwhelm.

5. Reconnect with Your "Why"
Remembering the reason you started your business can reignite your passion and provide clarity during challenging times. Take a step back and reflect on your initial motivation and goals.

6. Seek Support
Talking about your feelings and challenges can be cathartic. Consider joining entrepreneur support groups, hiring a business coach, or seeking therapy. Sometimes, merely vocalizing your struggles can bring solutions and relief.

7. Regularly Review & Adjust
Consistently assess your workload and responsibilities. As your business evolves, you might find that certain tasks or commitments no longer serve you or your company's mission. Don't be afraid to make changes.

Note on Work-Life Balance: One of the primary precursors to burnout is the blurring of lines between personal and professional time. As mentioned earlier, setting strict hours for work and availability not only helps in managing burnout but also in maintaining a healthy work-life balance. It reinforces the idea that while your business is crucial, it's only one facet of your life. Ensuring you have time for yourself, your health, and your loved ones can create a more harmonious balance, leading to greater satisfaction and success in all areas.

Remember, burnout isn't a sign of weakness; it's a sign that some elements in your professional or personal life need reassessment. By addressing burnout proactively, you're taking steps toward a more sustainable and successful entrepreneurial journey.

Business Quiz

Entrepreneurial Readiness Quiz

1. Why do you want to start a business?
A) I'm passionate about my idea and want to make a difference.
B) I want to be my own boss and have more flexibility.
C) It seems like a good way to make money.
D) Everyone else is doing it.

2. How do you handle failure?
A) I see it as a learning opportunity and move forward.
B) I get disappointed but try again.
C) I tend to avoid situations where I might fail.
D) I get discouraged and have a hard time moving on.

3. How do you handle uncertainty and risk?
A) I embrace it as part of the entrepreneurial journey.
B) I'm cautious but can deal with it when necessary.
C) I prefer stability and clear outcomes.
D) I avoid it at all costs.

4. How would you fund your business?
A) Savings, investors, and possibly loans.
B) Personal loans or credit cards.
C) I haven't thought about it yet.
D) Hopefully someone else will offer to pay for everything.

5. How do you handle feedback and criticism?
A) I actively seek it out and use it to improve.
B) It's tough, but I listen and try to learn from it.

C) I prefer not to get feedback unless it's positive.
D) I tend to get defensive or dismissive.

6. How well do you know your target market?
A) I've conducted research and have a clear understanding.
B) I have a general idea but need to do more research.
C) I think I know who they might be.
D) I haven't considered this yet.

7. Do you have a business plan or strategy?
A) Yes, I've outlined my business plan in detail.
B) I've started on one but haven't completed it.
C) No, but I know I need one.
D) I don't think I need one.

8. How do you handle stress and high-pressure situations?
A) I remain calm and find solutions to problems.
B) I get anxious but can manage.
C) I tend to avoid or delay dealing with them.
D) I easily get overwhelmed.

Results:
Mostly A's: You seem well-prepared for the entrepreneurial journey, equipped with the mindset and resources to navigate its challenges. Keep refining your skills and knowledge.
Mostly B's: You have a good foundation but may need more preparation in some areas. Consider seeking mentorship or further training.
Mostly C's: It's essential to address gaps in your readiness. Spend time researching, planning, and building resilience.
Mostly D's: Before diving into entrepreneurship, take time to educate yourself on business essentials and develop a growth mindset.

Building Resilience

Failure, as daunting as it sounds, is an inevitable part of the entrepreneurial journey. Every entrepreneur, from the most seasoned to the freshest face in the industry, has experienced failure in one form or another. What sets successful entrepreneurs apart is not the absence of failure, but their ability to learn from it, bounce back, and forge ahead with renewed determination. Here are some insights and tips to overcome failures and build resilience.

1. Change Your Perspective on Failure:
- Growth Mindset: Adopt a growth mindset. Instead of seeing failures as a reflection of your abilities, view them as opportunities to learn and grow.
- Failure as Feedback: Start seeing failure as feedback. It's information that tells you what's not working and pushes you to find what will.

2. Embrace the Lessons:
Every setback hides a lesson. Once the initial disappointment subsides, analyze what went wrong, what you could have done differently, and how you can prevent similar mistakes in the future.

3. Create a Support System:
- Network with Fellow Entrepreneurs: Sharing experiences and challenges with peers can provide both comfort and solutions.
- Seek Mentorship: Mentors, having been there and done that, can provide invaluable guidance and reassurance.
- Personal Support: Surrounding yourself with supportive family and friends can make a world of difference.

4. Set Realistic Expectations:
While ambition is crucial, setting unattainable goals can set you up for unnecessary disappointments. It's okay to aim high, but be ready to adapt and adjust your expectations based on real-world feedback.

5. Develop Emotional Intelligence (EQ):
A high EQ allows you to better manage your emotions, navigate stressful situations, empathize with others, and remain calm under pressure. It's a vital skill in bouncing back from setbacks.

6. Prioritize Self-Care:
Taking care of your mental and physical well-being ensures you have the energy and mindset to tackle challenges head-on. This includes proper sleep, regular exercise, and activities that rejuvenate you.

7. Celebrate Small Wins:
Every victory, no matter how small, is a step in the right direction. Celebrating them boosts morale, motivation, and reminds you of your capabilities.

8. Stay Flexible and Adapt:
Resilience also means flexibility. If one approach isn't working, be ready to pivot and adapt. Being rigid can result in unnecessary struggles and disappointments.

9. Limit Exposure to Negativity:
Whether it's negative people, news, or thoughts, limiting your exposure can help maintain a positive and proactive mindset.

10. Keep the Big Picture in Mind:
In the face of setbacks, remember why you started. Revisiting

your mission and vision can reignite your passion and drive.

In the end, resilience is not about avoiding failures but mastering the art of rebounding from them. It's a muscle, and the more you flex it, the stronger it becomes. Every challenge faced with grit and determination not only takes you one step closer to your business goals but also molds you into a more resilient and formidable entrepreneur. Remember, the most significant successes often come on the heels of failures. Embrace the journey, learn continuously, and let resilience be your guiding star.

Understanding Taxes

Navigating the complex landscape of business taxation can be daunting, but a basic understanding is crucial for every entrepreneur. Here's a simplified breakdown of what you need to know about taxes as a business owner in the U.S.:

1. Business Structure Determines Taxation:
Your business's legal structure determines how you will be taxed:

- Sole Proprietorship: The business income is treated as your personal income and is reported on your individual tax return using Schedule C.

- Partnerships: Partnerships file an information return (Form 1065). Individual partners report their share of the business's profit or loss on their personal tax returns.

- Corporations (C-Corp): They are separate tax entities and file a corporate tax return (Form 1120). They're subject to double taxation, where the corporation pays taxes on its net income, and shareholders also pay taxes on any dividends they receive.

- S-Corporations: They avoid double taxation. Income, deductions, and credits flow through to shareholders, who report these on their personal returns (Form 1120S).

- Limited Liability Companies (LLCs): The IRS can treat an LLC as a sole proprietorship, partnership, or a corporation, depending on circumstances and elections.

2. Income Tax:
Regardless of your business structure, you'll likely have to pay income tax. How and where you pay this depends on your business entity.

3. Self-Employment Tax:
If you're a sole proprietor, an LLC member, or a partner in a partnership, you're responsible for self-employment taxes (Medicare and Social Security) on your share of the business's profits.

4. Employment Taxes:
If you have employees, you're responsible for several additional taxes:

- Federal Income Tax Withholding: Employers need to withhold these taxes from their employees' wages.

- Social Security & Medicare Taxes: Employers deduct these from an employee's income and also match the amount as an employer contribution.

- Federal Unemployment Tax (FUTA): This tax is not deducted from the employee's wage but is an employer responsibility.

5. Excise Taxes:
These are taxes on specific products or services like gasoline, airline tickets, or tanning services. If your business deals with these goods/services, you might need to pay excise taxes.

6. Sales and Use Taxes:
If your state has a sales tax and you're selling tangible products or certain services, you'll need to collect, report, and remit these taxes.

7. Property Tax:
If your business owns property, you'll pay property tax. The amount varies by location and the property's assessed value.

8. Quarterly Estimated Taxes:
Most business owners must pay their taxes quarterly, rather than at the end of the year. These are estimated tax payments.

9. Recordkeeping:
Maintain meticulous records. Document all incomes, expenses, and any potential deductions. This will simplify tax preparation and protect you in case of an audit.

10. Consider Professional Guidance:
Given the complexity of business taxes, many entrepreneurs benefit from consulting with tax professionals. They can provide clarity, ensure compliance, and often identify tax-saving strategies.

Business Legal Compliance

Starting and running a business involves more than just a good idea and capital; it also requires a keen understanding of the legal obligations and protections that come with it. Ensuring that your business remains compliant with these rules will not only help in avoiding penalties but will also enhance your business's credibility.

Why is Legal Compliance Important?

1. Avoidance of Penalties: Non-compliance can lead to heavy fines and even potential jail time, depending on the violation.
2. Enhanced Reputation: Companies known for their adherence to legal standards tend to earn more respect in the market.
3. Reduced Litigation Risk: Compliant businesses have a reduced risk of lawsuits and other legal disputes.
4. Improved Operations: A legal framework can often streamline operations, ensuring that everything runs smoothly.

Business Legal Compliance Checklist:

1. Business Structure: Decide on the legal structure of your business (sole proprietorship, partnership, corporation, LLC, etc.). This decision will affect your registration requirements, liability, tax obligations, and other factors.

2. Business Name Registration: If your business name is different from your own name, you may need to register it with your state or local government.

3. Federal and State Tax IDs: Obtain an Employer Identification Number (EIN) from the IRS. Additionally, your state might require a state tax ID.

4. Licenses and Permits: These vary by industry, state, and municipality. Common ones include a business license, health department permit, and occupational permit.

5. Employment Laws: If you have employees, ensure you're compliant with state and federal labor laws, including wage and hour rules, anti-discrimination policies, and workplace safety regulations.

6. Zoning Laws: If you're opening a physical location, ensure your chosen site complies with local zoning laws.

7. Environmental Regulations: Depending on your business type, you may need to follow state or federal environmental regulations.

8. Advertising and Marketing Laws: Ensure that any advertisements, especially those for special groups like children, follow federal and state guidelines.

9. Online Business: If you conduct business online, understand e-commerce regulations, and ensure your business complies. These can relate to privacy, electronic payments, and more.

10. Insurance Depending on the nature of your business, you may require various insurances, such as general liability, professional liability, worker's compensation, and property insurance.

11. Intellectual Property: Consider protecting your business's unique ideas, products, or services with trademarks, patents, copyrights, or trade secrets.

12. Contracts: Ensure all business agreements are documented in well-drafted contracts, which could include partnership agreements, lease agreements, or client contracts.

13. Record Keeping: Maintain comprehensive records of all business transactions, including financial statements, tax filings, licenses, and other critical documents.

14. Periodic Renewals: Many permits and licenses require periodic renewals. Keep track of expiration dates and ensure timely renewals.

15. Stay Updated: Laws and regulations can change. Regularly review and update your compliance checklist to accommodate any new legal requirements.

Legal compliance is not just a requirement but also a strategy to ensure the smooth functioning of your business. While the above checklist covers many common requirements, it's crucial to consult with a legal expert to ensure comprehensive compliance specific to your business and location.

Powerful Digital Tools

In today's digital age, having the right tools at your fingertips can transform your business. They can save you time, reduce costs, and help present your brand professionally. Here's a curated list of must-have digital tools for the ambitious businesswoman:

1. Graphic Design & Branding:

- Canva: A user-friendly graphic design platform with templates for social media graphics, presentations, posters, and more. Even if you're not a design expert, Canva helps you create professional-grade visuals.

- Unsplash: A vast collection of high-quality, royalty-free photos. Perfect for your website, blog, or any other content needs.

- MidJourney: A platform for custom stock images, allowing you to find the perfect photo to represent your brand or message.

2. Content Generation & Writing:

- ChatGPT by OpenAI: An AI-driven tool that aids in content generation, from blog posts to business proposals. It's like having an assistant writer at your beck and call.

3. Website & E-commerce Platforms:

- Squarespace: A platform that offers visually appealing templates and a user-friendly interface for building professional websites. It's great for both beginners and those with some web design experience.

- Shopify: A top-tier e-commerce platform designed to make setting up an online store a breeze. It offers everything from payment processing to inventory management.

4. Task Management & Organization:

- Trello: A visual project management tool that uses boards and cards to organize tasks and track progress.

- Asana: A comprehensive project management tool suitable for bigger teams or projects, helping you stay on top of your to-do lists.

5. Communication:

- Slack: A messaging app designed for teams. It organizes conversations into channels, making it easier to collaborate on projects and streamline communications.

- Zoom: In the age of remote work, Zoom stands out as a reliable video conferencing tool, great for meetings, webinars, and online workshops.

6. Finance & Invoicing:

- QuickBooks: An accounting software that makes managing

finances, sending invoices, and tracking expenses more manageable.

- Wave: A free platform tailored for small business owners, freelancers, and consultants for accounting, invoicing, and payments.

7. Social Media Management:

- Buffer: Schedule, publish, and analyze all your posts in one place. It supports multiple social media platforms, ensuring your content reaches your audience at optimal times.

- Hootsuite: Another great tool for scheduling posts, monitoring social media, and analyzing results.

8. Learning & Skill Development:

- Udemy: An online learning platform with thousands of courses on everything from marketing to graphic design.

- Coursera: Offers courses in partnership with top universities and organizations worldwide.

9. Email Marketing:

- Mailchimp: An all-in-one email marketing tool that allows you to send newsletters, automate campaigns, and segment audiences.

10. Analytics:

- Google Analytics: Essential for anyone with a website, it provides insights into your site's traffic, audience behavior, and more.

In a rapidly evolving digital world, it's crucial to harness the right tools to stay ahead. By integrating these platforms into your daily operations, you can not only improve efficiency but also carve a niche and build a memorable brand. As you grow, keep an eye out for new tools and updates to existing ones, ensuring you're always at the forefront of your business game.

Always remember to look for alternative tools or platforms as the digital landscape is ever-evolving. While these tools offer great utility, always choose those that best suit your specific business needs and personal preferences.

Social Responsibility

In an increasingly connected world, businesses aren't just profit-driven entities; they play a critical role in shaping societal values and impacting the environment. As women entrepreneurs, integrating social and environmental responsibility can help create a brand that stands for more than just its products or services. Here's how you can lead with conscience and make a difference:

1. Understand Your Supply Chain:

- Sourcing responsibly: Partner with suppliers who have ethical labor practices. Ensure that the products or raw materials you're sourcing aren't linked to deforestation, overfishing, or other unsustainable practices.

- Transparency: Be open about where and how your products are made. A transparent supply chain can foster trust with your consumers.

2. Reduce, Reuse, Recycle:

- Eco-friendly packaging: Consider using biodegradable, compostable, or recyclable packaging. Many consumers are willing to pay a premium for eco-friendly products.

- Reduce waste: Audit your business processes to identify areas where waste can be minimized. Embrace digital documentation to reduce paper usage.

3. Support Women and Marginalized Communities:

- Hire diversely: Actively create job opportunities for underrepresented groups. This not only fosters diversity but also brings a broader range of perspectives to your business.

- Mentor and train: Offer mentorship or training programs to women and young girls interested in entrepreneurship.

4. Give Back:

- Community engagement: Identify local causes and nonprofits that align with your brand values and support them through donations or volunteering.

- Charitable partnerships: Launch products or campaigns where a percentage of sales goes to a specific cause.

5. Advocate for Green Practices:

- Eco-friendly office space: Use energy-efficient lighting, encourage carpooling or use of public transport among employees, and consider using renewable energy sources.

- Digital-first approach: Minimize physical outputs by taking advantage of digital platforms for marketing, communication, and product deliveries.

6. Stay Educated and Advocate:

- Continuous learning: Stay updated on the latest in sustainable practices and social issues. This not only benefits your business but also allows you to be a voice of influence in your community.

- Host events or workshops: Educate your consumers and community on the importance of sustainable and socially responsible practices.

7. Ethical Marketing:

- Authentic messaging: Ensure your marketing campaigns avoid greenwashing (providing misleading information about how a company's products are environmentally sound) and truly reflect your company's values and practices.

- Highlight social and environmental initiatives: Use your platform to raise awareness about causes you care about and the efforts your business is making.

Being socially and environmentally responsible isn't just a business strategy; it's a commitment to a larger purpose. By aligning your business with these values, you're not only setting it up for success but also playing a pivotal role in shaping a better world. As women entrepreneurs, the power to drive change is immense, and by leading with heart, purpose, and responsibility, the impact can be revolutionary.

Juggling Family & Business

For many women entrepreneurs, the challenge doesn't end with business plans, marketing strategies, or sales targets. It's the daily dance of balancing family life with business aspirations. How do you give your all to a business venture without feeling like you're shortchanging your family? Here are strategies and tips for successfully juggling both:

1. Prioritize & Plan:

- Set clear boundaries: Allocate specific times for work and family and stick to them as closely as possible. For example, avoid checking emails or taking business calls during family dinners.

- Use a planner or digital tools: Schedule both family and business commitments. This way, you won't double-book yourself and can visualize where your time is going.

2. Seek Support:

- Family involvement: Communicate with your family about your business goals. When they understand the 'why' behind your work, they're more likely to support and even help when they can.

- Hire help: Consider hiring assistance for certain household tasks or using childcare services if needed. It can free up time and reduce stress.

3. Learn to Say 'No':

- Set realistic expectations: You can't be everywhere at once. It's okay to decline additional responsibilities that don't align with your current priorities.

- Delegate tasks: In both business and family life, trust others to handle certain responsibilities. You don't have to do it all.

4. Quality Over Quantity:

- Focused family time: Make the moments you spend with family count. Engage in activities everyone enjoys and be present in the moment.

- Efficient work hours: When it's time to work, reduce distractions and be as productive as possible. This way, you can accomplish more in less time.

5. Self-care is Essential:

- Schedule personal time: Just as you would a business meeting, schedule time for self-care. A refreshed mind and body can handle challenges better.

- Find hobbies outside work and family: Engaging in activities just for yourself can help in maintaining a balanced perspective.

6. Flexibility is Key:

- Adapt to changes: Some days might not go as planned. Instead of stressing, adjust and realign your schedule.

- Evaluate regularly: What worked for your family and business balance a month ago might not work today. Regularly reassess and make changes as needed.

7. Celebrate Small Wins:

- Acknowledge effort: Celebrate the small victories, whether it's a successful business deal or your child's achievement at school.

- Stay positive: Instead of focusing on what you couldn't do, appreciate what you managed to achieve.

Balancing family and business is a continuous journey of learning and adapting. While it can be overwhelming at times, remember that both spheres of your life enrich you in different ways. With communication, planning, and a good support system, you can flourish in both roles, ensuring neither gets left behind.

Business Glossary

1. Accounts Payable (A/P): Amounts owed by a company to suppliers for goods and services received.

2. Accounts Receivable (A/R): Amounts owed to a company by its customers for goods or services provided on credit.

3. Angel Investor: A private individual who provides capital to startups in exchange for ownership equity or convertible debt.

4. Assets: Anything of value that a business owns, including cash, accounts receivable, inventory, property, and other tangible and intangible items.

5. Balance Sheet: A financial statement that displays a company's assets, liabilities, and shareholders' equity at a specific point in time.

6. Break-Even Point: The point at which total revenue equals total costs, resulting in neither profit nor loss.

7. Business-to-Business (B2B): Companies that sell products or services directly to other businesses, rather than consumers.

8. Business-to-Consumer (B2C): Companies that sell products or services directly to individual consumers.

9. Capital: The financial assets, such as funds held in deposit accounts and funds obtained from special financing sources, used by entrepreneurs and businesses to buy what they need to make their products or provide their services.

10. Cash Flow: A measure of a company's financial health, indicating the net amount of cash and cash equivalents flowing in and out of a business.

11. Depreciation: The method of allocating costs to the appropriate period. Although the physical object is often intact, the value of an asset is reduced over time.

12. Elevator Pitch: A brief, persuasive speech used to spark interest in what your organization does.

13. Equity: The ownership interest of shareholders in a business, calculated by subtracting liabilities from assets.

14. Franchise: A system in which entrepreneurs purchase the rights to open and operate a business from a larger corporation.

15. Gross Profit: The profit a company makes after deducting the costs associated with making and selling its products.

16. Incorporate: The act of forming a new corporation, which is recognized as a separate entity from its owners.

17. Liabilities: The amounts a company owes to others, such as loans, accounts payable, mortgages, accrued expenses, etc.

18. Liquidity: The ease with which an asset can be converted into cash.

19. Market Capitalization: The total dollar market value of a company's outstanding shares of stock.

20. Net Income: The total profit of a company, calculated by subtracting total expenses from total revenues.

21. Operating Expenses: Expenses a business incurs as a result of its normal business operations, including salaries, rent, utilities, etc.

22. Profit Margin: A measure of profitability calculated by dividing net income by revenue.

23. Return on Investment (ROI): A performance measure used to evaluate the efficiency of an investment or compare the efficiency of different investments.

24. Startup: A new business in the initial stages of operations.

25. Venture Capital: A form of private equity and a type of financing that investors provide to startup companies and small businesses with long-term growth potential.

26. Wholesale: Selling of goods in large quantities, typically for resale.

27. Working Capital: The capital of a business used in its day-to-day operations, calculated as current assets minus current liabilities.

Made in United States
North Haven, CT
25 August 2023